10

PARALLEL PARADISE

story and art
LYNN OKAMOTO

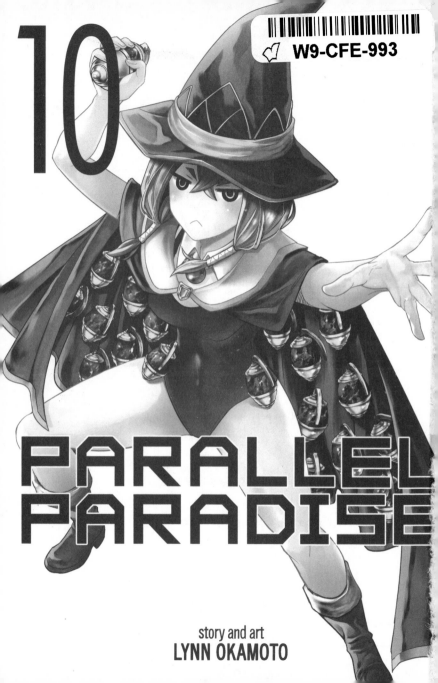

CONTENTS

Chapter 91 Inadequate!

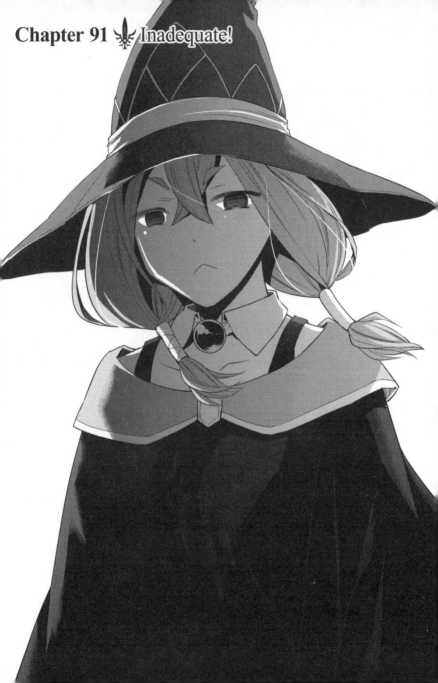

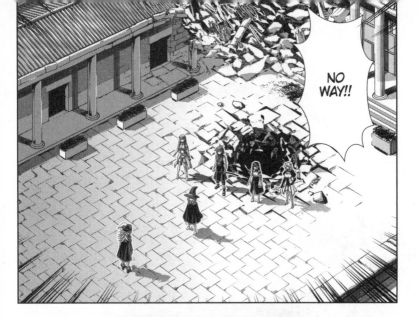

NO WAY!!

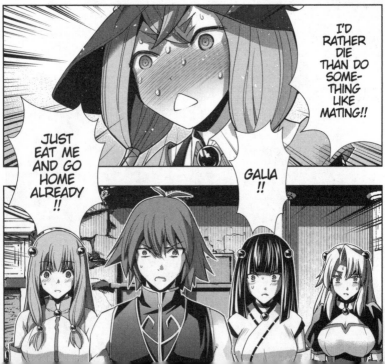

I'D RATHER DIE THAN DO SOMETHING LIKE MATING!!

JUST EAT ME AND GO HOME ALREADY!!

GALIA!!

EAT ME !!
...
HEH HEH HEH ...
HEH HEH HEH ...
HOW INTEREST-ING.

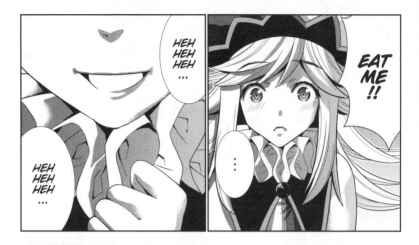

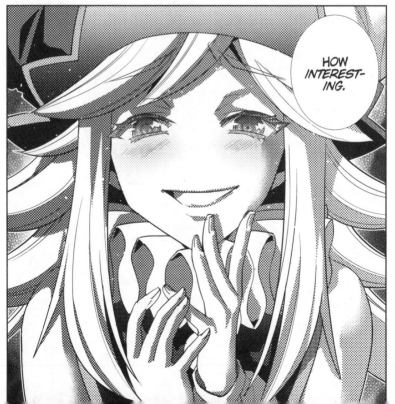

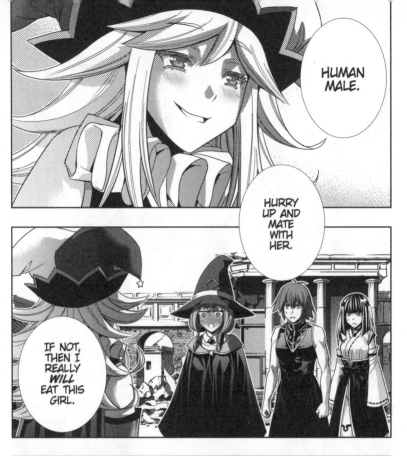

HUMAN MALE.

HURRY UP AND MATE WITH HER.

IF NOT, THEN I REALLY *WILL* EAT THIS GIRL.

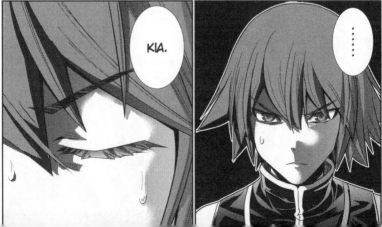

KIA.

. . . . .

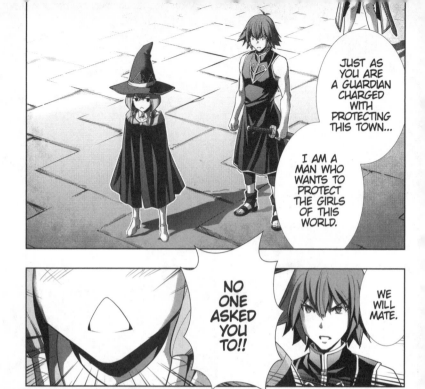

JUST AS YOU ARE A GUARDIAN CHARGED WITH PROTECTING THIS TOWN...

I AM A MAN WHO WANTS TO PROTECT THE GIRLS OF THIS WORLD.

WE WILL MATE.

NO ONE ASKED YOU TO!!

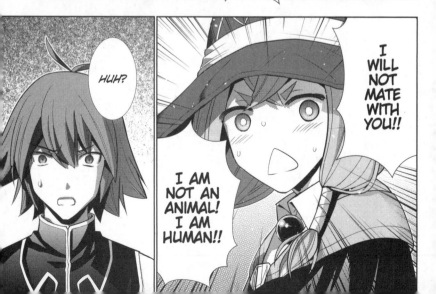

HUH?

I WILL NOT MATE WITH YOU!!

I AM NOT AN ANIMAL! I AM HUMAN!!

SCRRAPE
ザッ
SCRRAPE
ザッ
SCRRAPE
ザッ
SCRRAPE
ザッ
OINK
ブヒッ
OINK
ブヒッ
OINK
ブヒッ

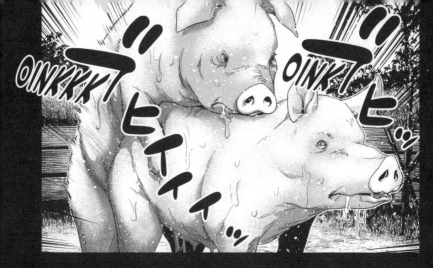

OINKKK

OINK

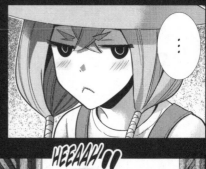

DISGUST-ING.

...

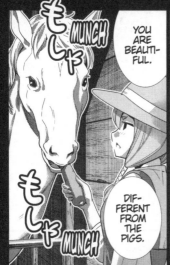

MUNCH

MUNCH

YOU ARE BEAUTI-FUL.

DIF-FERENT FROM THE PIGS.

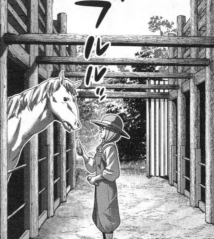

HEEAAH!

MOVE, KIA.
IT'S TIME TO BREED THEM.
HEAHAHA

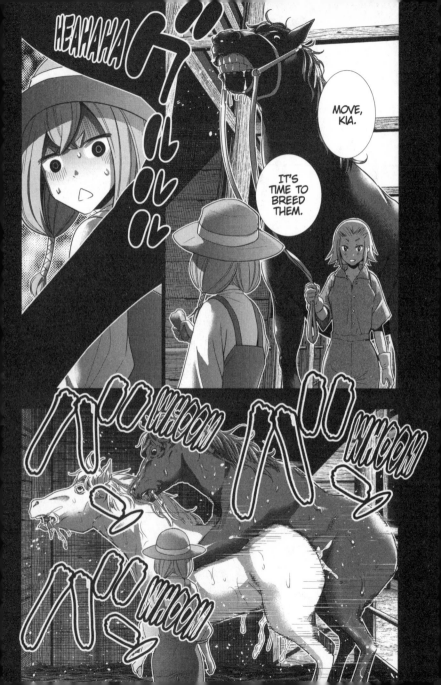

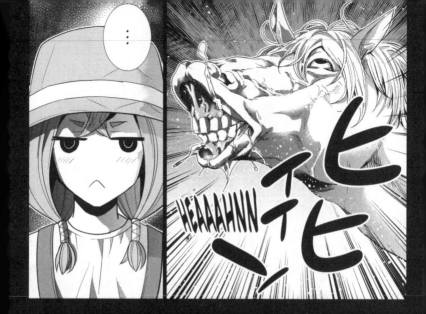

HEAAAHNN

SO
DISGUSTING.

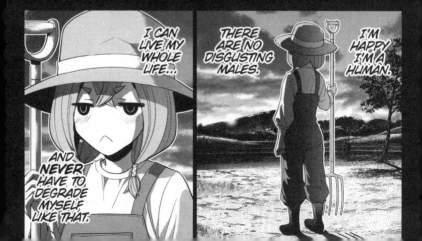

I CAN LIVE MY WHOLE LIFE...

AND NEVER HAVE TO DEGRADE MYSELF LIKE THAT.

THERE ARE NO DISGUSTING MALES.

I'M HAPPY I'M A HUMAN.

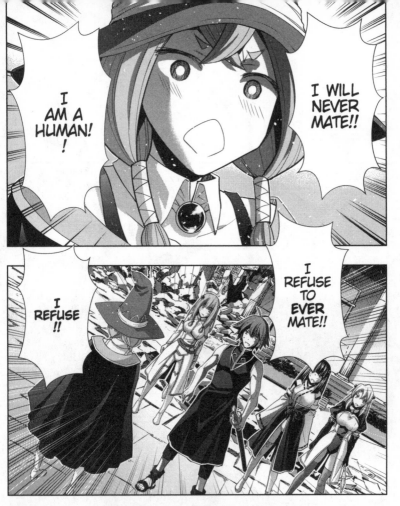

I AM A HUMAN!!

I WILL NEVER MATE!!

I REFUSE!!

I REFUSE TO EVER MATE!!

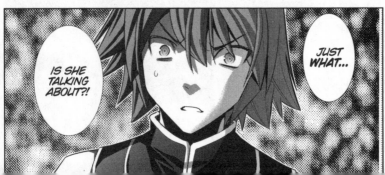

IS SHE TALKING ABOUT?!

JUST WHAT...

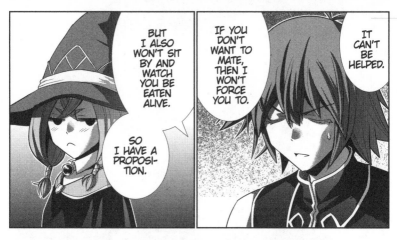

BUT I ALSO WON'T SIT BY AND WATCH YOU BE EATEN ALIVE.

SO I HAVE A PROPOSI-TION.

IF YOU DON'T WANT TO MATE, THEN I WON'T FORCE YOU TO.

IT CAN'T BE HELPED.

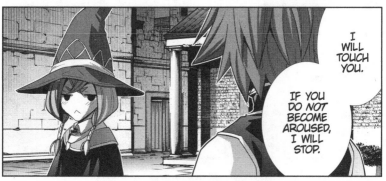

I WILL TOUCH YOU.

IF YOU DO *NOT* BECOME AROUSED, I WILL STOP.

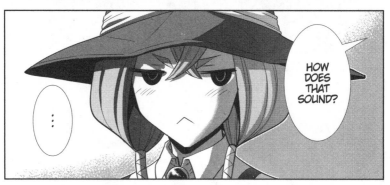

...

HOW DOES THAT SOUND?

13

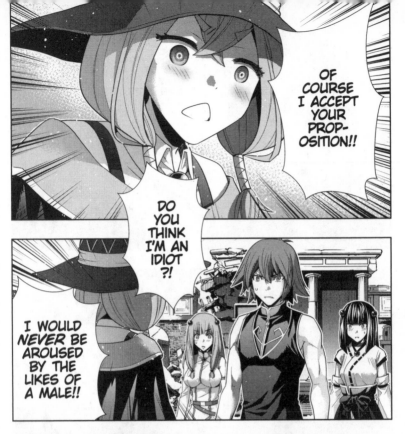

OF COURSE I ACCEPT YOUR PROP- OSITION!!

DO YOU THINK I'M AN IDIOT ?!

I WOULD *NEVER* BE AROUSED BY THE LIKES OF A MALE!!

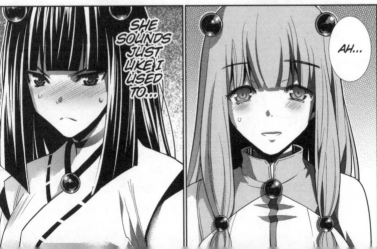

SHE SOUNDS JUST LIKE I USED TO...

AH...

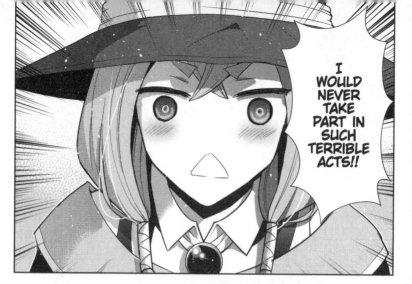

I WOULD NEVER TAKE PART IN SUCH TERRIBLE ACTS!!

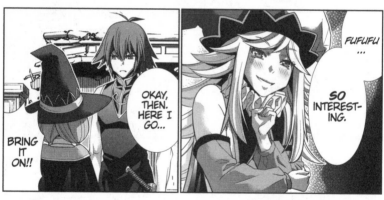

OKAY, THEN. HERE I GO...

BRING IT ON!!

FUFUFU...

SO INTERESTING.

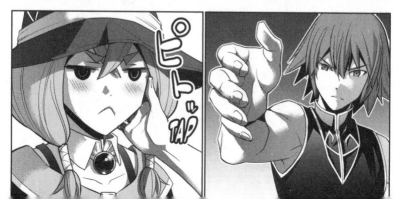

ピトッ TAP

バチ
SHOCK
バチ
SHOCK
バチ
SHOCK

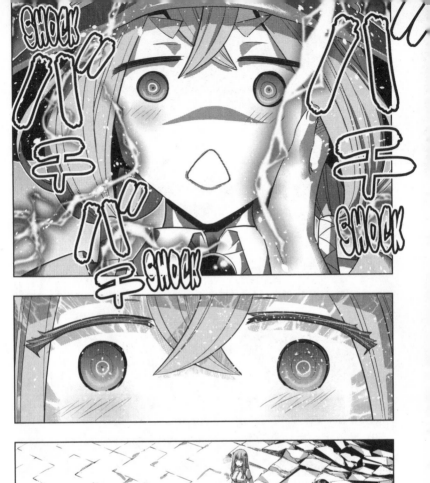

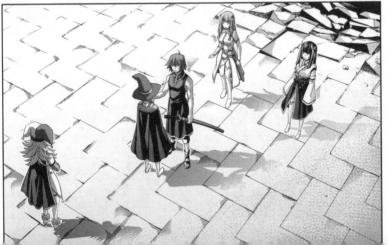

...
HUH?
パ
SLAP
HUH?!
...
I WIN.

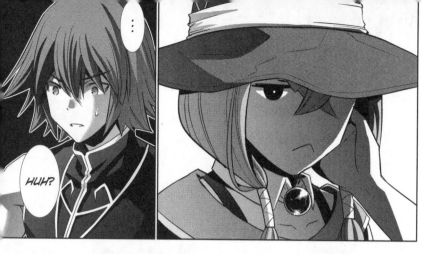

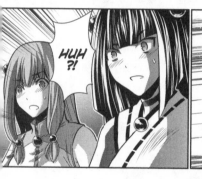

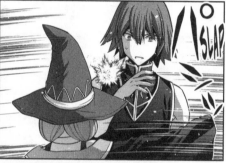

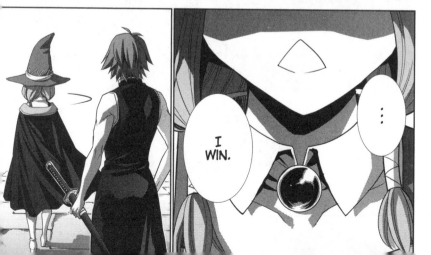

OH WELL.

I GUESS I WILL HELP MYSELF THEN.

...

TMP カッ

TMP カッ

NO WAY!!

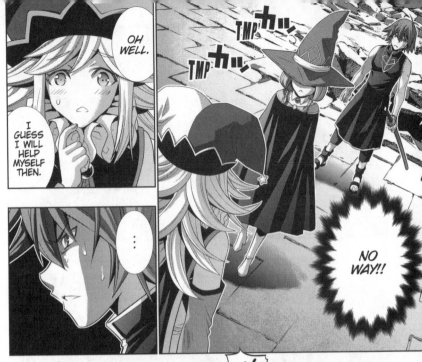

HAHH!

HAHHH!

I'D BE LUCKY IF I COULD EVEN MANAGE A SWING. WORST-CASE SCENARIO, I'M DEAD ON THE SPOT.

I HAVE NO WAY OF DEFEATING GALIA.

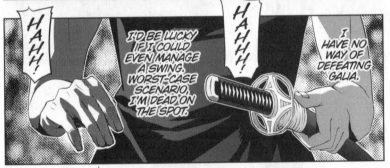

HAHHH!

JUST LET KIA BE KILLED.

BUT I CANNOT...

HAHH!

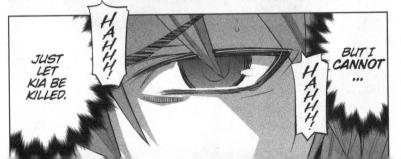

KIA
!!
THUDD

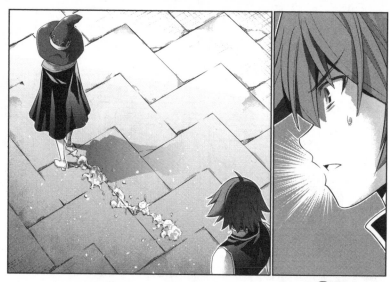

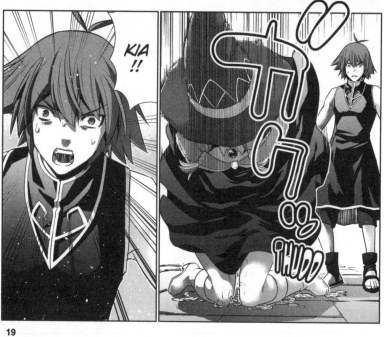

HAHH!
HAHH!
SHPLURT
くっちゅ
SHPLURT
くっちゅ
HAHH!
…
THAT'S THE SAME KIA WHO ABSOLUTELY REFUSED TO MATE...
AHH!
HAHH!
くっちゅ
SHPLURT
くっちゅ
SHPLURT
ビュルビュル
SHPLOOSH
SHPLOOSH
NOW SHE HAS BEGUN TO TOUCH HERSELF...
AHHHHH!
AHHHHH!

Chapter 92 Kill La Kia

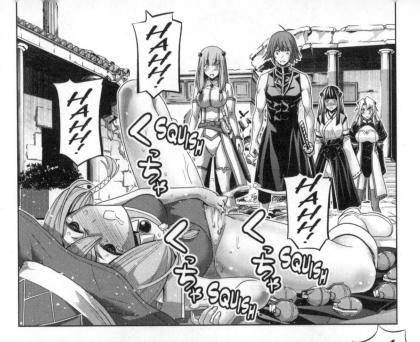

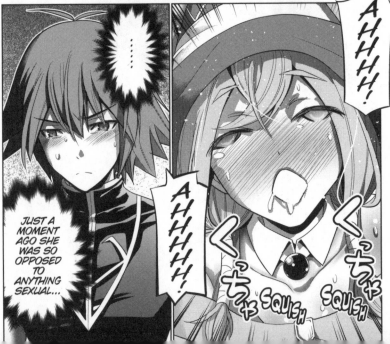

JUST A MOMENT AGO SHE WAS SO OPPOSED TO ANYTHING SEXUAL...

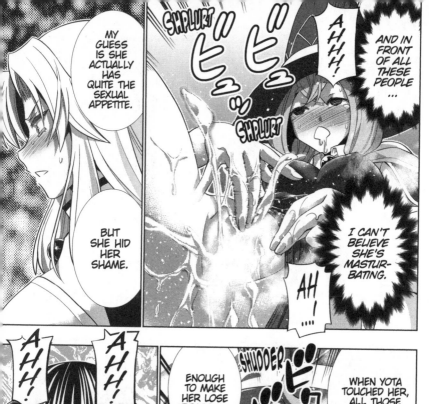

MY GUESS IS SHE ACTUALLY HAS QUITE THE SEXUAL APPETITE.

BUT SHE HID HER SHAME.

SHPLURT

ピュー ピュー

SHPLURT

AHH!

AND IN FRONT OF ALL THESE PEOPLE...

I CAN'T BELIEVE SHE'S MASTURBATING.

AH!....

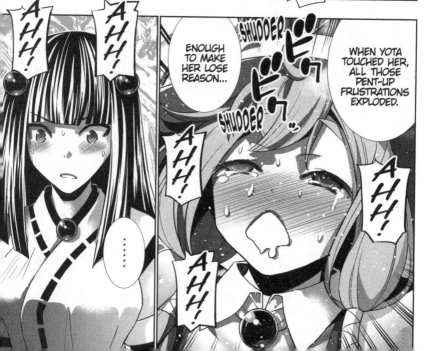

AHH!

AHH!

ENOUGH TO MAKE HER LOSE REASON...

....

SHUDDER

ビクッ

ビクッ

SHUDDER

WHEN YOTA TOUCHED HER, ALL THOSE PENT-UP FRUSTRATIONS EXPLODED.

AHH!

AHH!

AHH!

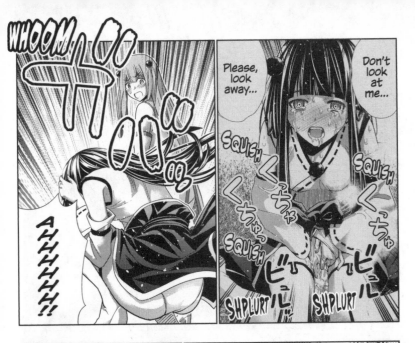

WHOOM

AHHHHHH!!

Please, look away...

Don't look at me...

SQUISH

SQUISH

SQUISH

SHPLURT

SHPLURT

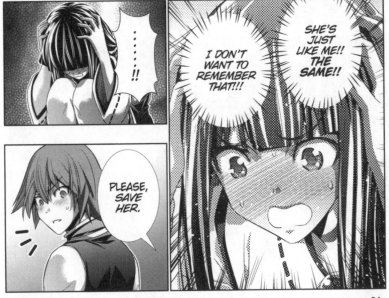

......

!!

PLEASE, SAVE HER.

I DON'T WANT TO REMEMBER THAT!!!

SHE'S JUST LIKE ME!! THE SAME!!

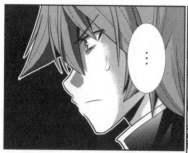

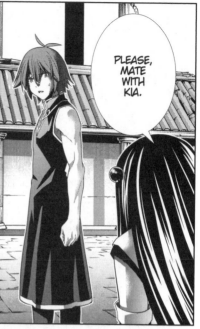

PLEASE, MATE WITH KIA.

:

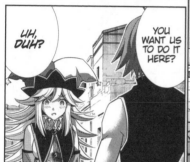

UH, DUH?

YOU WANT US TO DO IT HERE?

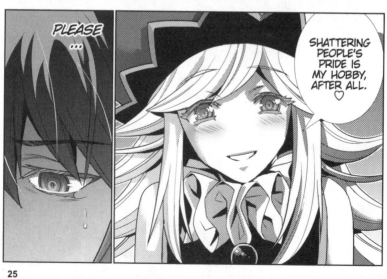

PLEASE ...

SHATTERING PEOPLE'S PRIDE IS MY HOBBY, AFTER ALL. ♡

SHE ALREADY HAS NO PRIDE LEFT.
PLEASE...
I WANT YOU TO...
ビュルルッ
SHPLURRRR
ビュルルッ
SHPLURRRR
I BETTER NOT PUSH HER ANY FURTHER OR GALIA MIGHT TRY TO PUT SOMETHING STRANGE UP HER BUTT AGAIN.
I'LL FINISH THIS NOW.
チャキ
SHINK
THIS IS BORING.
HER PRIDE IS ALREADY LONG GONE.
?!
GIVE ME A BREAK!!

NEVER MIND, YOU DON'T HAVE TO MATE WITH HER.
?!
ACTUALLY, YOU'RE NOT *ALLOWED* TO MATE WITH HER.
HAHHHH!
OBEY THAT, AND I WILL LET YOU OFF THE HOOK TODAY.
HAHHHH!
...
LUCKY !!
HAHHHH!
HAHHHH!
NOOOOOO!!

PUCKER
ぱぁ
ビュッ
SHPLURT
SHPLURT
ビュビュッ
SHPLURT
PUT IT IN!!
I WANT YOU TO!!
PLEASE!!
I WANT TO!!
WEREN'T YOU JUST SAYING THAT YOU'D NEVER MATE?
HOW UNSIGHTLY YOU HUMANS ARE...

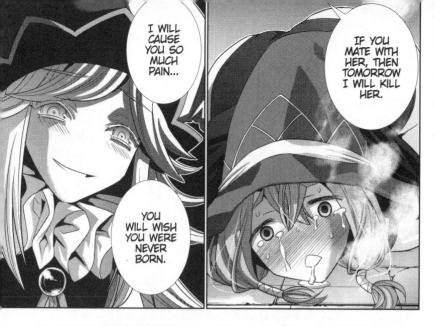

I WILL CAUSE YOU SO MUCH PAIN...

IF YOU MATE WITH HER, THEN TOMORROW I WILL KILL HER.

YOU WILL WISH YOU WERE NEVER BORN.

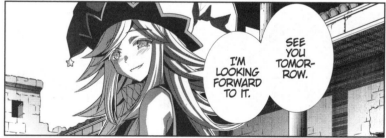

I'M LOOKING FORWARD TO IT.

SEE YOU TOMORROW.

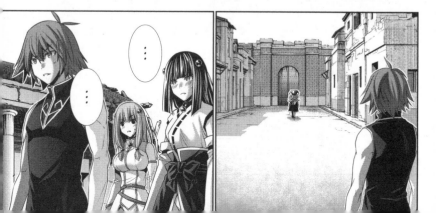

...

...

CLENCH
DO IT...
HAHH!
HAHH!
SQUISH
SQUISH
I WANT YOU TO...
SQUISH
YOU ...!!
DID YOU NOT HEAR HER?!
MATE ...
MATE ...
THUD
OOMF!!

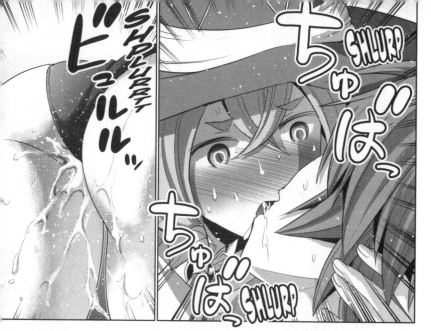

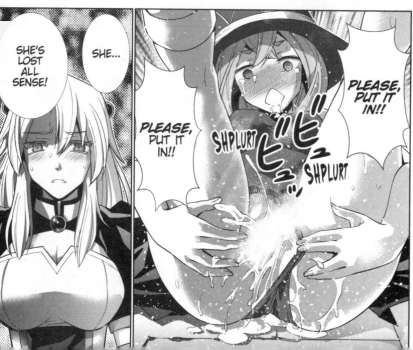

SHE'S LOST ALL SENSE!

SHE...

PLEASE, PUT IT IN!!

PLEASE, PUT IT IN!!

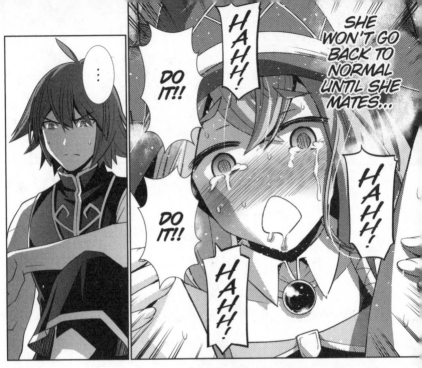

SHE WON'T GO BACK TO NORMAL UNTIL SHE MATES...

DO IT!!

HAHH!

DO IT!!

HAHH!

HAHH!

HAHH!

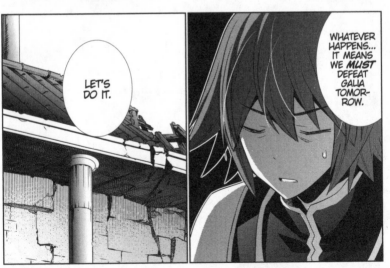

WHATEVER HAPPENS... IT MEANS WE *MUST* DEFEAT GALIA TOMOR-ROW.

LET'S DO IT.

SHLUP
WAAAAAAHHHHH!!
SHLAP
HAHH!
HAHH!
SHLAP
HAHH!
SHLAP

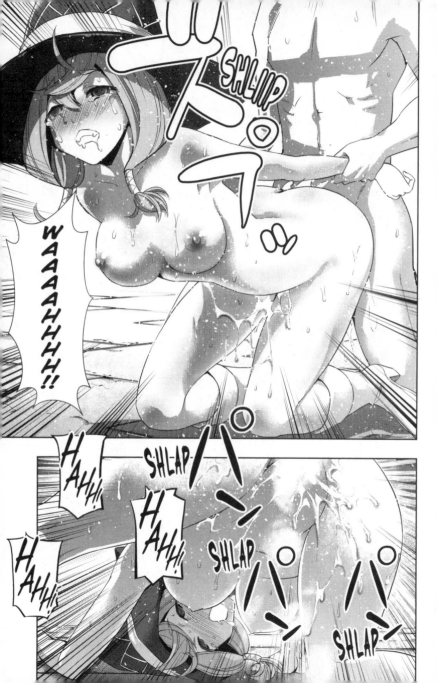

AHHHHH!
SHLAP
AHHHHH!
SHPEWW
SHLAP
SHLAP
YESS!!
THAT FEELS AMAZING!!
I'M JUST LIKE AN ANIMAL!!
I KNEW IT! I'M JUST AN ANIMAL!!
SHLAP
AHHH!
SHLAP
SHLAP
AHHH!

AHH!
AHH!
I'M JUST A FEMALE...
WHO LOSES HER MIND OVER THE SLIGHTEST TOUCH OF A MALE!!
AHH!
I'M JUST AN ANIMAL!! NO DIFFERENT!!
JUST AN ANIMAL WHO CAN ONLY THINK ABOUT MATING!!
ANGHH!
ANGHH!
びゃる
SHPLURT
びゃるっ
SHPLURT
HAHH!
HAHH!
HUHHH!
HUHHH!
くっちゃ
SHPEWW
くっちゃ
SHPEWW

YEEESS!!
YOU SURE ARE A LOUD ONE.
SHPEW
SHPEW
ANNGGHHHHH!!
SHLAP
SHLAP
SHLAP
MY GOD!!
YOU ARE AN ANIMAL!!
YOU ARE EVEN PUTTING MATING BEFORE YOUR OWN LIFE!!
GYA-HH-HH!!
SHLAP
SHPLURTTT
SHLAP

AHNNNN!
MMMMH!!
HEHHHH!
I KNOW MY WORDS ARE REACHING HER.
HAHH!
SHPLURT
じゅるっ
SHLURP
ちゅばっ
HAHHH!
ちゅばっ
SHLURP
HAHHH!
じゅるるる
SHLURRRP
AH-HH-HH!
YET SHE STILL DOESN'T WANT TO STOP.
SHLAP
パンッ
SHLAP
パンッ
SHLAP
パンッ
SHLAP
パンッ

SHQUIRT
I'M GOING TO COME!!
I'M GOING TO COME!!
SHQUIRT
GIVE ME YOUR SPERM!!
SHPLURT
IMPREGNATE ME LIKE AN ANIMAL!!
SHPLURT
THEN HOW ABOUT YOU COME LIKE AN ANIMAL RIGHT IN FRONT OF EVERYONE?
SHLAP
SHLAP
SHLAP
DRIBBLE
DRIBBLE
SHOOM
SHOOM
I'M GOING TO COME! I'M GOING TO COME! COME ...!

DRIBBLE
I KNEW IT...
DRIBBLE
DRIBBLE
AHH-HHH!
I AM JUST A BEAST CON-TROLLED BY HER SEX DRIVE.
SHPLURT
SHUDDER
CHOKE!

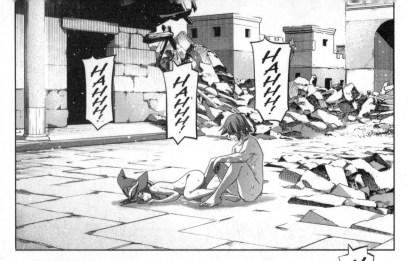

HAHHH! HAHHH! HAHHH! HAHHH!

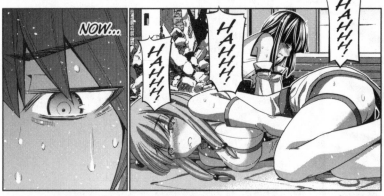

NOW...

HAHHH! HAHHH! HAHHH!

WE HAVE
NO CHOICE
BUT TO
DEFEAT GALIA
TOMORROW.

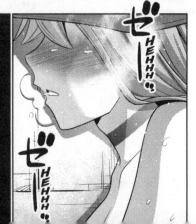

HEHHH!!

HEHHH!!

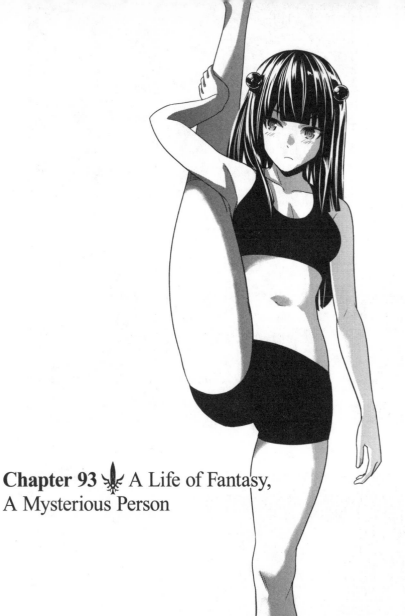

Chapter 93 A Life of Fantasy,
A Mysterious Person

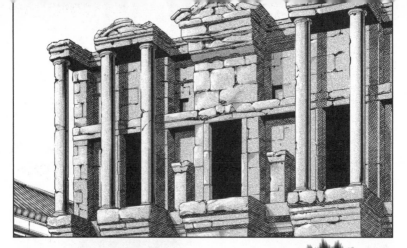

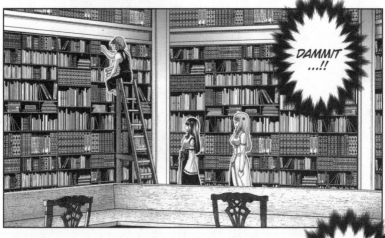

DAMMIT
...!!

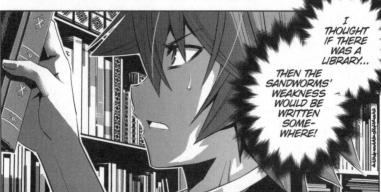

I THOUGHT IF THERE WAS A LIBRARY... THEN THE SANDWORMS' WEAKNESS WOULD BE WRITTEN SOME- WHERE!

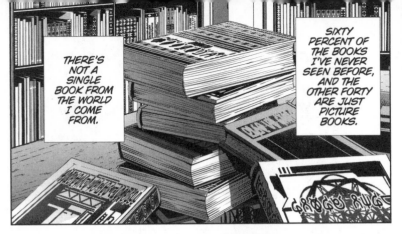

THERE'S NOT A SINGLE BOOK FROM THE WORLD I COME FROM.

SIXTY PERCENT OF THE BOOKS I'VE NEVER SEEN BEFORE, AND THE OTHER FORTY ARE JUST PICTURE BOOKS.

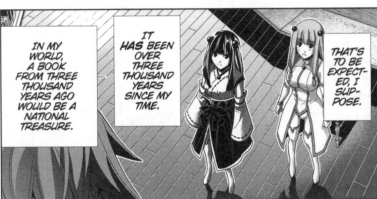

IN MY WORLD, A BOOK FROM THREE THOUSAND YEARS AGO WOULD BE A NATIONAL TREASURE.

IT HAS BEEN OVER THREE THOUSAND YEARS SINCE MY TIME.

THAT'S TO BE EXPECTED, I SUPPOSE.

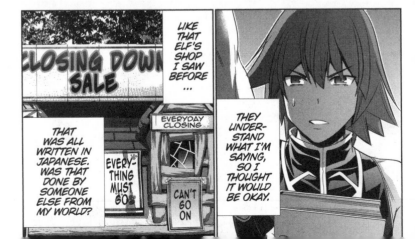

LIKE THAT ELF'S SHOP I SAW BEFORE...

CLOSING DOWN SALE

EVERYDAY CLOSING

EVERYTHING MUST GO!

CAN'T GO ON

THAT WAS ALL WRITTEN IN JAPANESE. WAS THAT DONE BY SOMEONE ELSE FROM MY WORLD?

THEY UNDERSTAND WHAT I'M SAYING, SO I THOUGHT IT WOULD BE OKAY.

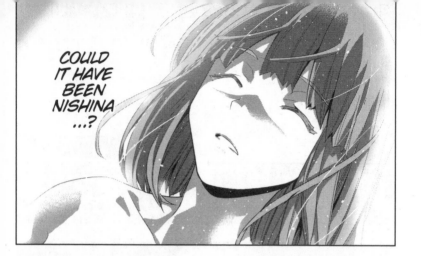

COULD IT HAVE BEEN NISHINA ...?

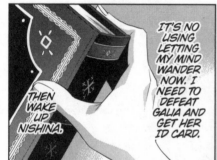

THEN WAKE UP, NISHINA.

IT'S NO USING LETTING MY MIND WANDER NOW. I NEED TO DEFEAT GALIA AND GET HER ID CARD.

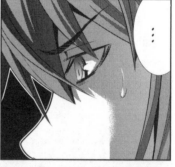

:

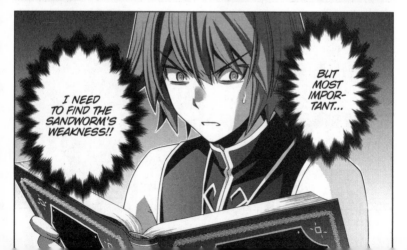

I NEED TO FIND THE SANDWORM'S WEAKNESS!!

BUT MOST IMPOR-TANT...

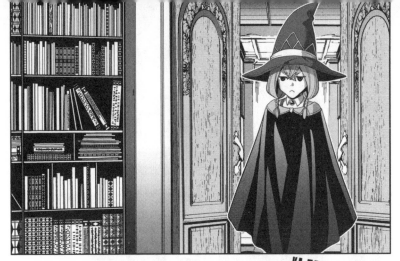

I SHOULD BE ABLE TO TELL WHICH IS A BOOK ABOUT MONSTERS.

EVEN IF I CAN'T READ...

パラ FLIP
FLIP パラ

KA-TAP

カタ

I WILL HELP.

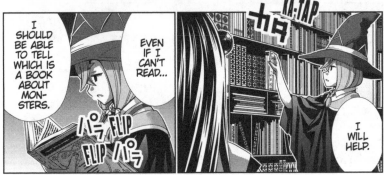

WE WILL HELP TOO.

⋮

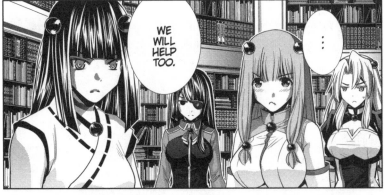

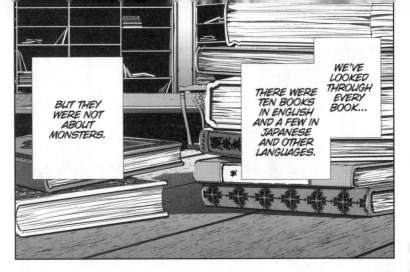

BUT THEY WERE NOT ABOUT MONSTERS.

THERE WERE TEN BOOKS IN ENGLISH AND A FEW IN JAPANESE AND OTHER LANGUAGES.

WE'VE LOOKED THROUGH EVERY BOOK...

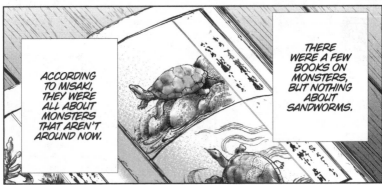

ACCORDING TO MISAKI, THEY WERE ALL ABOUT MONSTERS THAT AREN'T AROUND NOW.

THERE WERE A FEW BOOKS ON MONSTERS, BUT NOTHING ABOUT SANDWORMS.

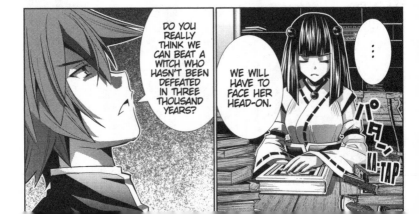

DO YOU REALLY THINK WE CAN BEAT A WITCH WHO HASN'T BEEN DEFEATED IN THREE THOUSAND YEARS?

WE WILL HAVE TO FACE HER HEAD-ON.

:

KA-TAP

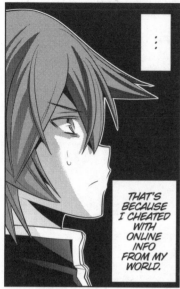

:

That's because I cheated with online info from my world.

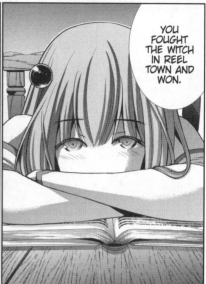

You fought the witch in Reel Town and won.

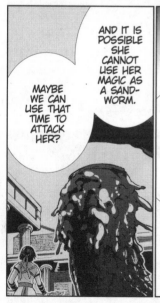

Maybe we can use that time to attack her?

And it is possible she cannot use her magic as a sand-worm.

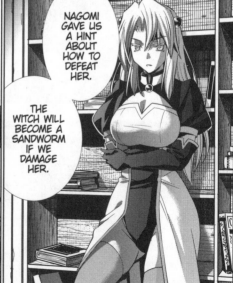

Nagomi gave us a hint about how to defeat her.

The witch will become a sandworm if we damage her.

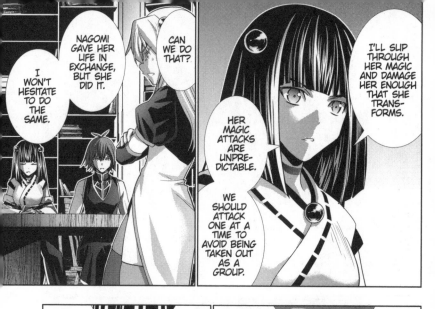

I WON'T HESITATE TO DO THE SAME.

NAGOMI GAVE HER LIFE IN EXCHANGE, BUT SHE DID IT.

CAN WE DO THAT?

I'LL SLIP THROUGH HER MAGIC AND DAMAGE HER ENOUGH THAT SHE TRANSFORMS.

HER MAGIC ATTACKS ARE UNPREDICTABLE.

WE SHOULD ATTACK ONE AT A TIME TO AVOID BEING TAKEN OUT AS A GROUP.

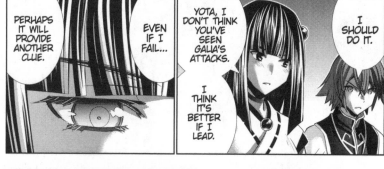

PERHAPS IT WILL PROVIDE ANOTHER CLUE.

EVEN IF I FAIL...

YOTA, I DON'T THINK YOU'VE SEEN GALIA'S ATTACKS.

I THINK IT'S BETTER IF I LEAD.

I SHOULD DO IT.

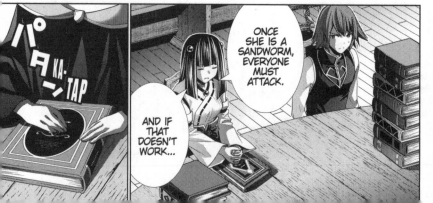

パ
ヵ KA-
ー TAP

ONCE SHE IS A SANDWORM, EVERYONE MUST ATTACK.

AND IF THAT DOESN'T WORK...

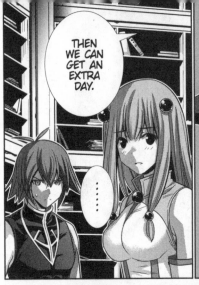

THEN WE CAN GET AN EXTRA DAY.

......

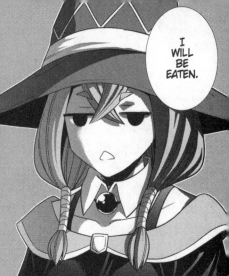

I WILL BE EATEN.

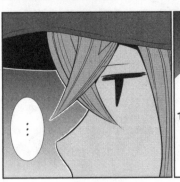

...

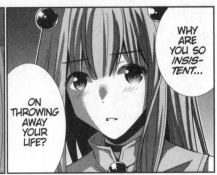

WHY ARE YOU SO INSISTENT...

ON THROWING AWAY YOUR LIFE?

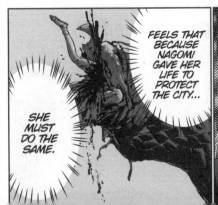

FEELS THAT BECAUSE NAGOMI GAVE HER LIFE TO PROTECT THE CITY...

SHE MUST DO THE SAME.

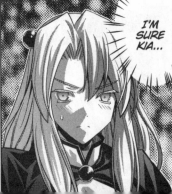

I'M SURE KIA...

I REFUSE.

I WILL NOT ALLOW YOU TO THROW AWAY YOUR LIFE LIKE THAT.

I DON'T CARE.

GALIA SAID SHE WOULD MAKE YOU SUFFER SO MUCH, YOU'D WISH YOU WERE NEVER BORN.

I REFUSE TO LET THAT HAPPEN.

TAP
ポン

IT'S WHAT I DESERVE FOR BEING SWALLOWED UP BY MOMENTARY PLEASURES.

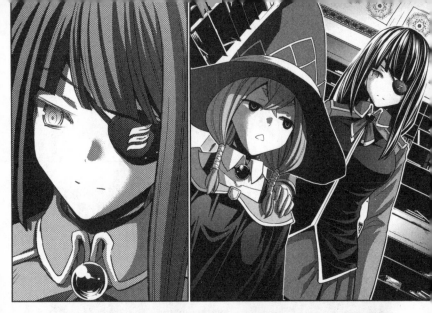

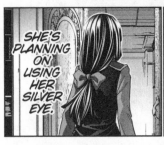

SHE'S PLANNING ON USING HER SILVER EYE.

AMANE...

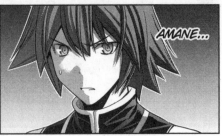

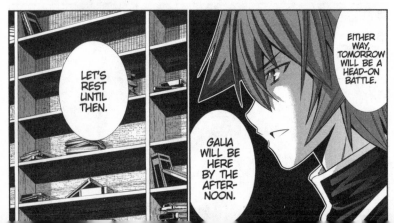

EITHER WAY, TOMORROW WILL BE A HEAD-ON BATTLE.

LET'S REST UNTIL THEN.

GALIA WILL BE HERE BY THE AFTER-NOON.

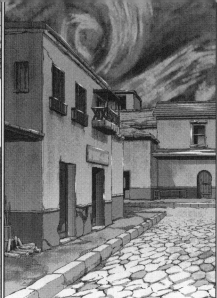

THIS ROOM ...

IT SURE HAS BEEN A WHILE.

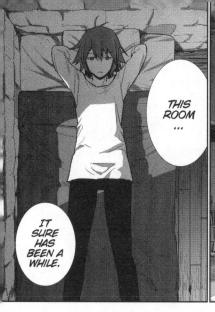

:

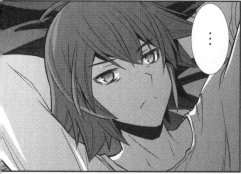

SURE BRINGS ME BACK...

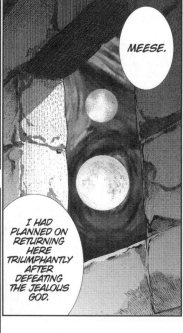

MEESE.

I HAD PLANNED ON RETURNING HERE TRIUMPHANTLY AFTER DEFEATING THE JEALOUS GOD.

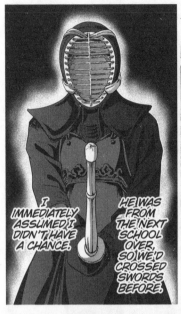

I IMMEDIATELY ASSUMED I DIDN'T HAVE A CHANCE.

HE WAS FROM THE NEXT SCHOOL OVER, SO WE'D CROSSED SWORDS BEFORE.

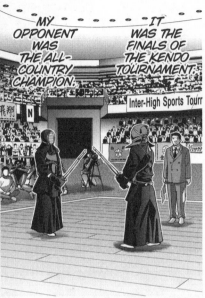

MY OPPONENT WAS THE ALL-COUNTRY CHAMPION.

IT WAS THE FINALS OF THE KENDO TOURNAMENT.

Inter-High Sports Tourn

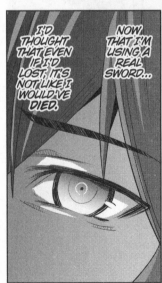

I'D THOUGHT THAT EVEN IF I'D LOST, IT'S NOT LIKE I WOULD'VE DIED.

NOW THAT I'M USING A REAL SWORD...

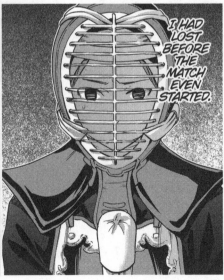

I HAD LOST BEFORE THE MATCH EVEN STARTED.

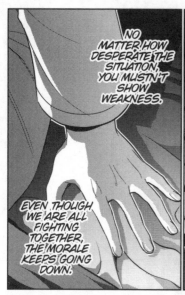

NO MATTER HOW DESPERATE THE SITUATION, YOU MUSTN'T SHOW WEAKNESS.

EVEN THOUGH WE ARE ALL FIGHTING TOGETHER, THE MORALE KEEPS GOING DOWN.

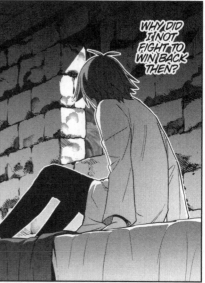

WHY DID I NOT FIGHT TO WIN BACK THEN?

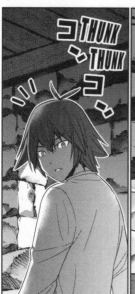

コ THUNK

THUNK コ

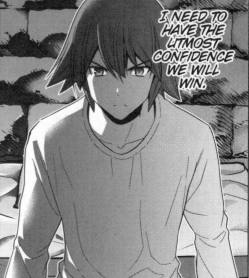

I NEED TO HAVE THE UTMOST CONFIDENCE WE WILL WIN.

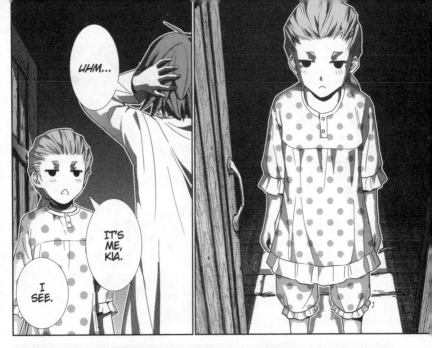

UHM...

IT'S ME, KIA.

I SEE.

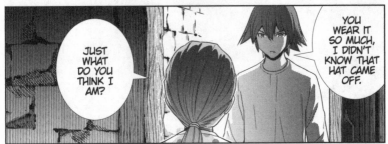

JUST WHAT DO YOU THINK I AM?

YOU WEAR IT SO MUCH, I DIDN'T KNOW THAT HAT CAME OFF.

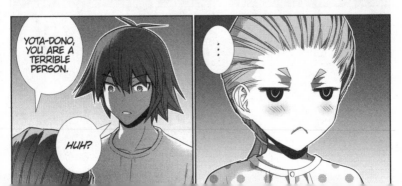

YOTA-DONO, YOU ARE A TERRIBLE PERSON.

HUH?

...

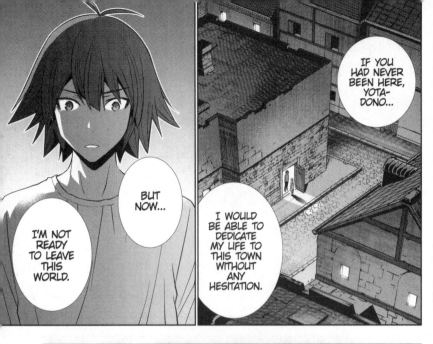

IF YOU HAD NEVER BEEN HERE, YOTA-DONO...

I WOULD BE ABLE TO DEDICATE MY LIFE TO THIS TOWN WITHOUT ANY HESITATION.

BUT NOW...

I'M NOT READY TO LEAVE THIS WORLD.

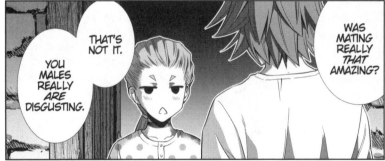

WAS MATING REALLY *THAT* AMAZING?

THAT'S NOT IT.

YOU MALES REALLY *ARE* DISGUSTING.

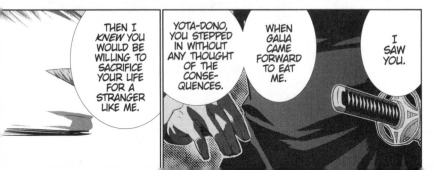

THEN I *KNEW* YOU WOULD BE WILLING TO SACRIFICE YOUR LIFE FOR A STRANGER LIKE ME.

YOTA-DONO, YOU STEPPED IN WITHOUT ANY THOUGHT OF THE CONSEQUENCES.

WHEN GALIA CAME FORWARD TO EAT ME.

I SAW YOU.

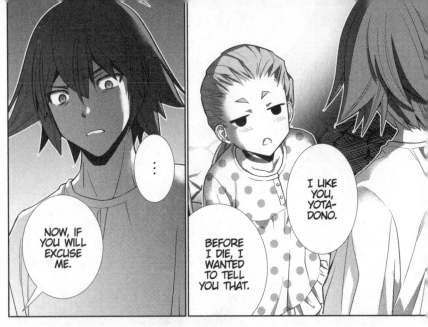

: . .

NOW, IF YOU WILL EXCUSE ME.

BEFORE I DIE, I WANTED TO TELL YOU THAT.

I LIKE YOU, YOTA-DONO.

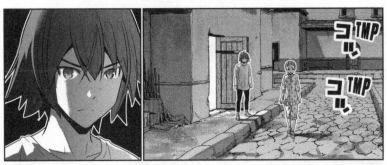

TMP

TMP

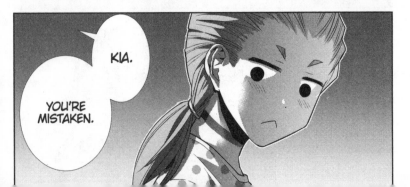

KIA.

YOU'RE MISTAKEN.

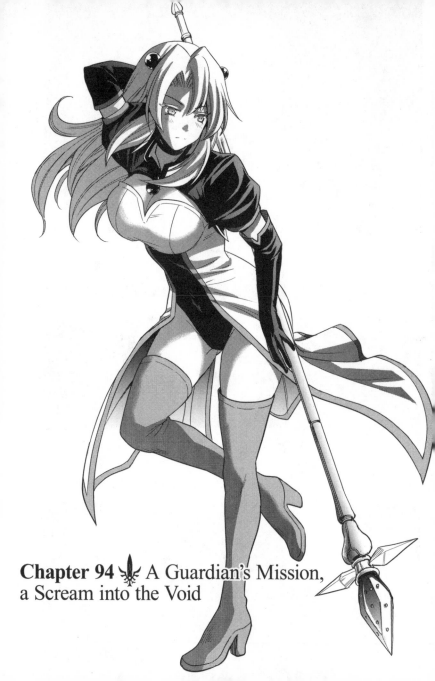

Chapter 94 ⚜ A Guardian's Mission, a Scream into the Void

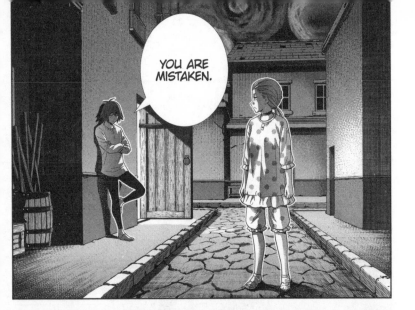

YOU ARE MISTAKEN.

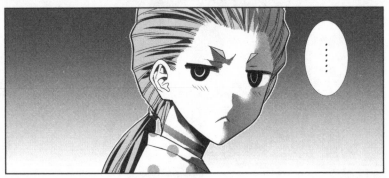

. . . . .

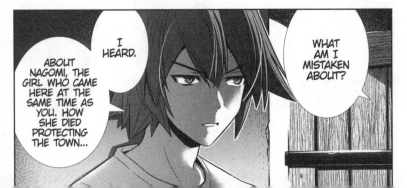

WHAT AM I MISTAKEN ABOUT?

I HEARD.

ABOUT NAGOMI, THE GIRL WHO CAME HERE AT THE SAME TIME AS YOU. HOW SHE DIED PROTECTING THE TOWN...

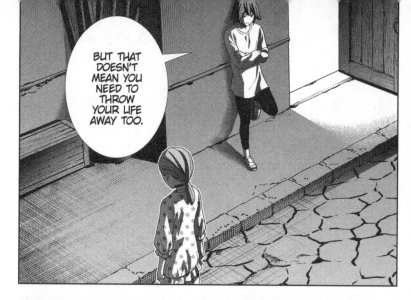

BUT THAT DOESN'T MEAN YOU NEED TO THROW YOUR LIFE AWAY TOO.

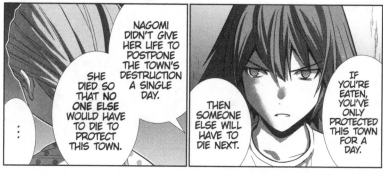

SHE DIED SO THAT NO ONE ELSE WOULD HAVE TO DIE TO PROTECT THIS TOWN.

NAGOMI DIDN'T GIVE HER LIFE TO POSTPONE THE TOWN'S DESTRUCTION A SINGLE DAY.

THEN SOMEONE ELSE WILL HAVE TO DIE NEXT.

IF YOU'RE EATEN, YOU'VE ONLY PROTECTED THIS TOWN FOR A DAY.

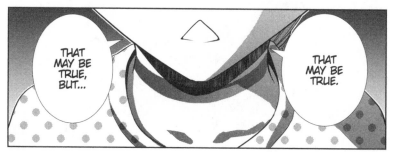

THAT MAY BE TRUE, BUT...

THAT MAY BE TRUE.

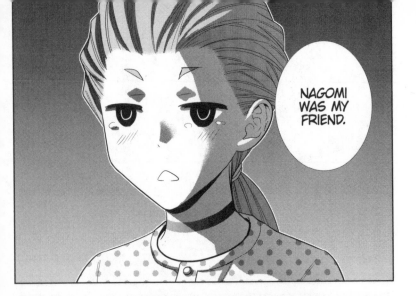

NAGOMI WAS MY FRIEND.

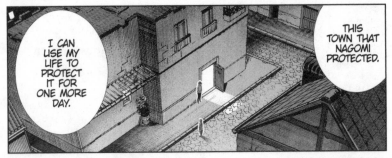

THIS TOWN THAT NAGOMI PROTECTED.

I CAN USE MY LIFE TO PROTECT IT FOR ONE MORE DAY.

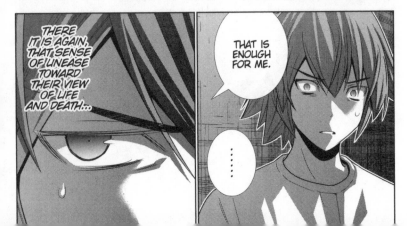

THERE IT IS AGAIN, THAT SENSE OF UNEASE TOWARD THEIR VIEW OF LIFE AND DEATH...

THAT IS ENOUGH FOR ME.

. . . . .

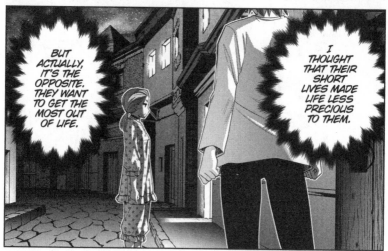

BUT ACTUALLY, IT'S THE OPPOSITE. THEY WANT TO GET THE MOST OUT OF LIFE.

I THOUGHT THAT THEIR SHORT LIVES MADE LIFE LESS PRECIOUS TO THEM.

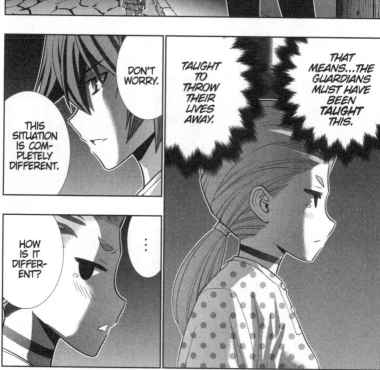

DON'T WORRY.

THIS SITUATION IS COMPLETELY DIFFERENT.

HOW IS IT DIFFERENT?

TAUGHT TO THROW THEIR LIVES AWAY.

THAT MEANS...THE GUARDIANS MUST HAVE BEEN TAUGHT THIS.

BECAUSE I'M HERE NOW.
...
YOU SOUND CONFI-DENT.
OF COURSE I DO.
LIKE THEY SAY, SICK-NESS AND HEALTH BEGIN IN YOUR MIND.
?
OR PERHAPS I SHOULD SAY: "WHERE THERE'S A WILL, THERE'S A WAY!"

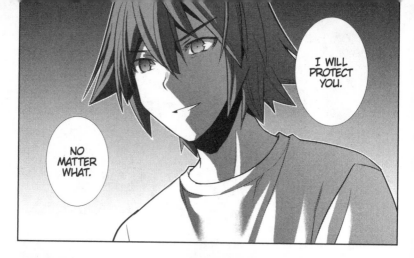

I WILL PROTECT YOU.

NO MATTER WHAT.

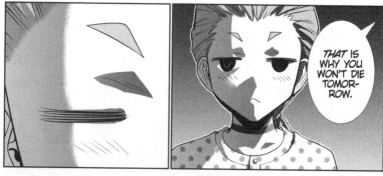

THAT IS WHY YOU WON'T DIE TOMORROW.

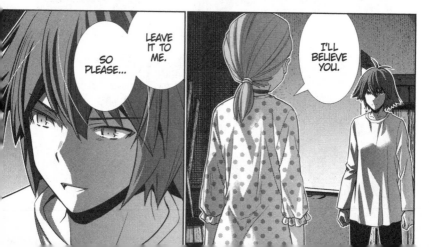

LEAVE IT TO ME.

SO PLEASE...

I'LL BELIEVE YOU.

DON'T THINK THAT YOU NEED TO MATE ONCE MORE BEFORE YOU DIE.
?!
W-W-WHAT!! WHO ARE YOU?!
I N-N-NEVER SAID I CAME HERE TO MATE!!
LIAR.
YOU'VE LEFT A SLIMY TRAIL BEHIND YOU LIKE A SLUG.
!!!!!!!!!!!!
AHHHHHH!!
YOU WON'T BE DYING TOMORROW, SO WE WILL NOT BE MATING TONIGHT.

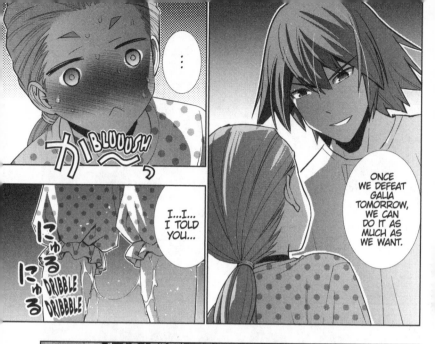

ONCE WE DEFEAT GALIA TOMORROW, WE CAN DO IT AS MUCH AS WE WANT.

I...I... I TOLD YOU...

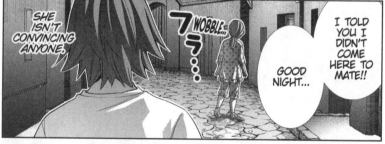

SHE ISN'T CONVINCING ANYONE.

WOBBLE...

GOOD NIGHT...

I TOLD YOU I DIDN'T COME HERE TO MATE!!

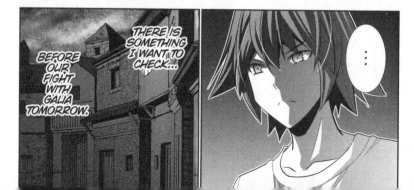

BEFORE OUR FIGHT WITH GALIA TOMORROW.

THERE IS SOMETHING I WANT TO CHECK...

:

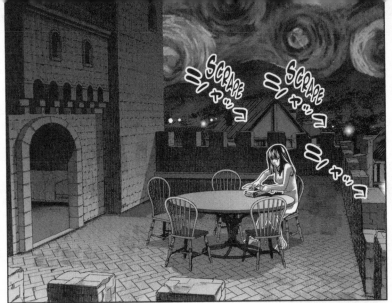

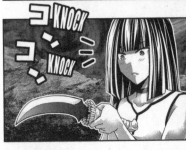

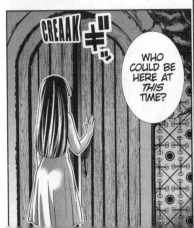

WHO COULD BE HERE AT *THIS* TIME?

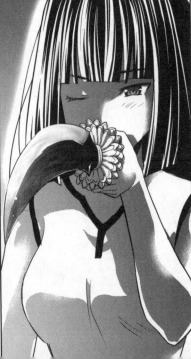

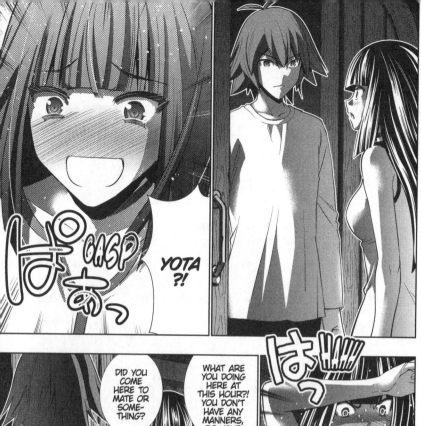

GASP

YOTA ?!

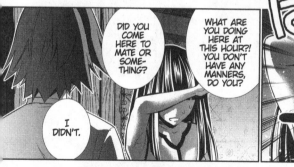

DID YOU COME HERE TO MATE OR SOMETHING?

WHAT ARE YOU DOING HERE AT THIS HOUR?! YOU DON'T HAVE ANY MANNERS, DO YOU?

I DIDN'T.

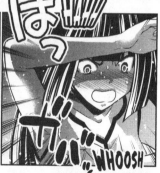

WHOOSH

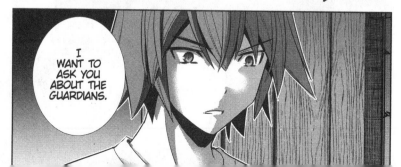

I WANT TO ASK YOU ABOUT THE GUARDIANS.

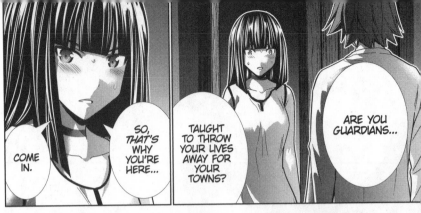

COME IN.

SO, THAT'S WHY YOU'RE HERE...

TAUGHT TO THROW YOUR LIVES AWAY FOR YOUR TOWNS?

ARE YOU GUARDIANS...

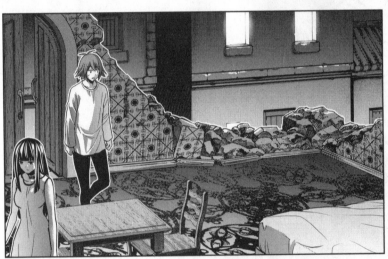

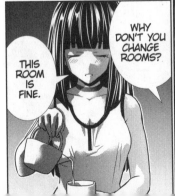

WHY DON'T YOU CHANGE ROOMS?

THIS ROOM IS FINE.

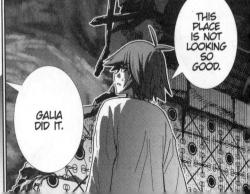

THIS PLACE IS NOT LOOKING SO GOOD.

GALIA DID IT.

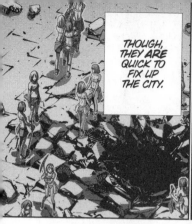

THOUGH, THEY ARE QUICK TO FIX UP THE CITY.

THEY JUST LEAVE BROKEN THINGS AS THEY ARE.

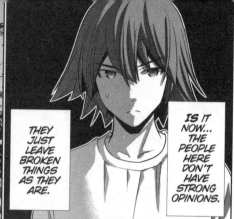

IS IT NOW... THE PEOPLE HERE DON'T HAVE STRONG OPINIONS.

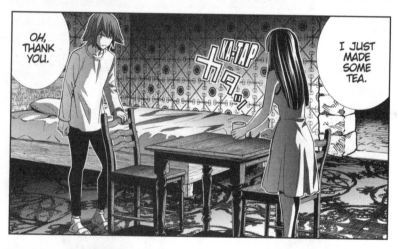

OH, THANK YOU.

KA-TAP

I JUST MADE SOME TEA.

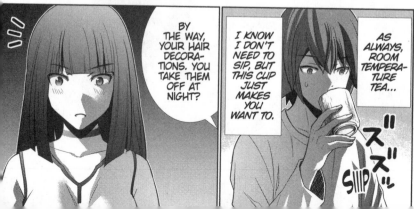

BY THE WAY, YOUR HAIR DECORATIONS. YOU TAKE THEM OFF AT NIGHT?

I KNOW I DON'T NEED TO SIP, BUT THIS CUP JUST MAKES YOU WANT TO.

AS ALWAYS, ROOM TEMPERATURE TEA...

ズズ
SIIIP

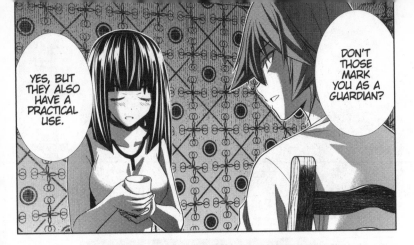

YES, BUT THEY ALSO HAVE A PRACTICAL USE.

DON'T THOSE MARK YOU AS A GUARDIAN?

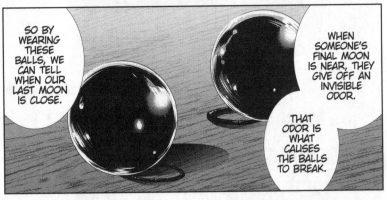

SO BY WEARING THESE BALLS, WE CAN TELL WHEN OUR LAST MOON IS CLOSE.

WHEN SOMEONE'S FINAL MOON IS NEAR, THEY GIVE OFF AN INVISIBLE ODOR.

THAT ODOR IS WHAT CAUSES THE BALLS TO BREAK.

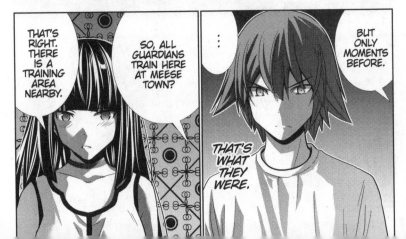

THAT'S RIGHT. THERE IS A TRAINING AREA NEARBY.

SO, ALL GUARDIANS TRAIN HERE AT MEESE TOWN?

: :

BUT ONLY MOMENTS BEFORE.

THAT'S WHAT THEY WERE.

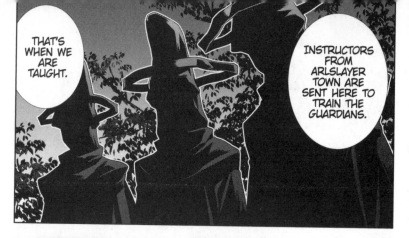

THAT'S WHEN WE ARE TAUGHT.

INSTRUCTORS FROM ARLSLAYER TOWN ARE SENT HERE TO TRAIN THE GUARDIANS.

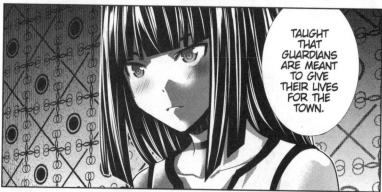

TAUGHT THAT GUARDIANS ARE MEANT TO GIVE THEIR LIVES FOR THE TOWN.

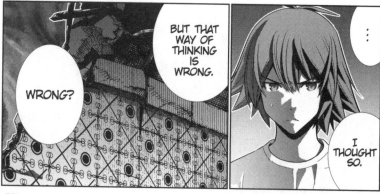

BUT THAT WAY OF THINKING IS WRONG.

WRONG?

:

I THOUGHT SO.

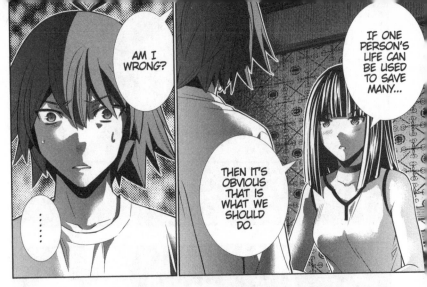

AM I WRONG?

IF ONE PERSON'S LIFE CAN BE USED TO SAVE MANY...

THEN IT'S OBVIOUS THAT IS WHAT WE SHOULD DO.

· · · · ·

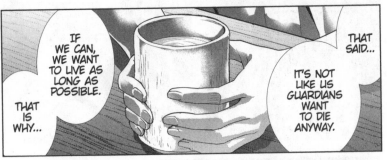

IF WE CAN, WE WANT TO LIVE AS LONG AS POSSIBLE.

THAT IS WHY...

THAT SAID...

IT'S NOT LIKE US GUARDIANS WANT TO DIE ANYWAY.

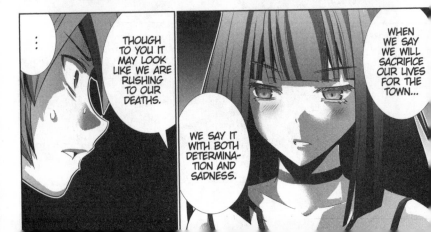

:

THOUGH TO YOU IT MAY LOOK LIKE WE ARE RUSHING TO OUR DEATHS.

WE SAY IT WITH BOTH DETERMINA- TION AND SADNESS.

WHEN WE SAY WE WILL SACRIFICE OUR LIVES FOR THE TOWN...

YET... NO MATTER WHAT WORLD YOU'RE IN, RISKING YOUR LIFE FOR SOMEONE IS NOT AN EASY THING.

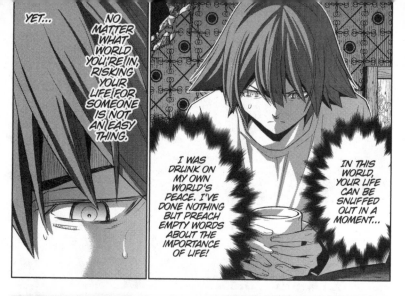

I WAS DRUNK ON MY OWN WORLD'S PEACE. I'VE DONE NOTHING BUT PREACH EMPTY WORDS ABOUT THE IMPORTANCE OF LIFE!

IN THIS WORLD, YOUR LIFE CAN BE SNUFFED OUT IN A MOMENT...

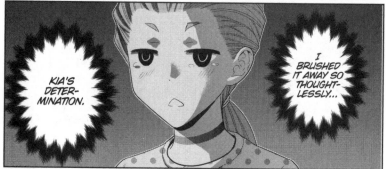

KIA'S DETERMINATION.

I BRUSHED IT AWAY SO THOUGHTLESSLY...

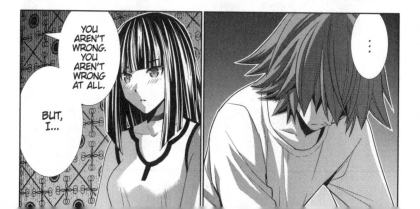

YOU AREN'T WRONG. YOU AREN'T WRONG AT ALL.

BUT, I...

:

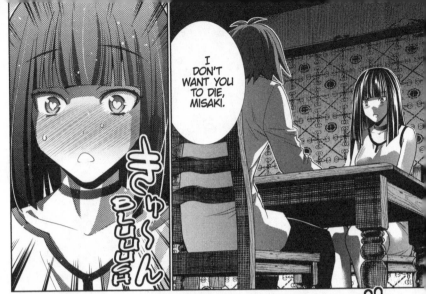

I DON'T WANT YOU TO DIE, MISAKI.

きゃ～ん BLUUUSH

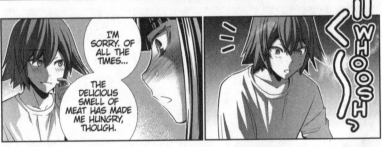

I'M SORRY. OF ALL THE TIMES...

THE DELICIOUS SMELL OF MEAT HAS MADE ME HUNGRY, THOUGH.

く WHOOSH

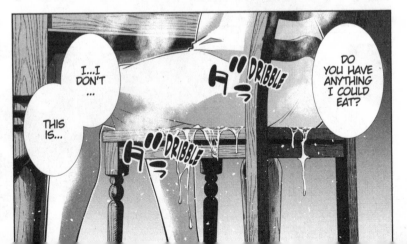

I...I DON'T...

THIS IS...

DRIBBLE

DRIBBLE

DO YOU HAVE ANYTHING I COULD EAT?

Chapter 95 Groovy / Gloomy

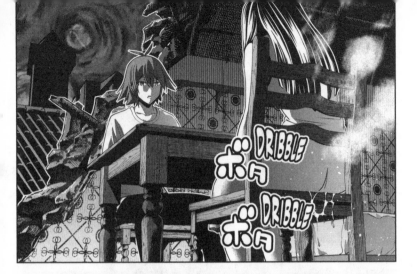

DRIBBLE
ボタ

DRIBBLE
ボタ

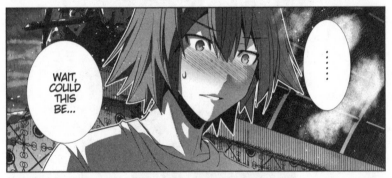

WAIT, COULD THIS BE...

. . . . .

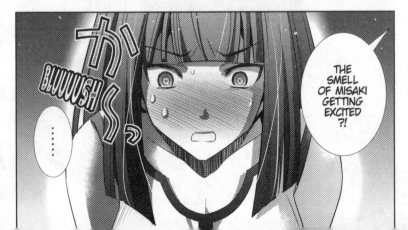

BLUUUSH

THE SMELL OF MISAKI GETTING EXCITED?!

. . . . .

DO YOU FIND ME APPALLING?
WHAT?
TOMOR-ROW... WE MAY ALL DIE, YET...
HERE I AM, BLATANTLY AROUSED. DO YOU NOT FIND ME APPALL-ING?
HAHH!
HAHH!
HAHH!
...
HOW COULD I?
ガタ
KER-TAP

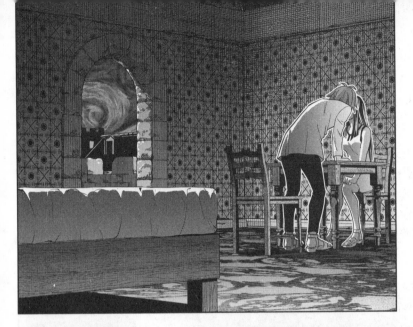

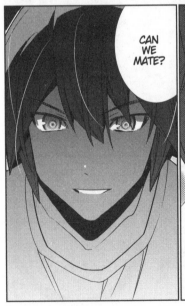

CAN WE MATE?

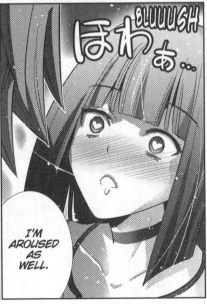

BLUUUSH

ほわぁ…

I'M AROUSED AS WELL.

KA-TAP
SHLURRP
じゅるるるっ
SHLURRP
じゅるるるっ
SHLURP
ちゅぱっ
SHLURP
ちゅぱっ
SHLURP
HAHHH!
HAHHH!
WHAT HAS YOU SO EAGER?
I'M GOING TO FINISH.
HAHHH!
HAHHH!
ゴプッ
GLUBB
GULP
ゴクン
HAHHH!
じゅるるっ
SHLURRRP

SHLURRP
ペチャッ
SHLURRP
ペチャッ
SHPLURT
ぴゅるっ
SHPLURT
ぴゅるっ
SHLURRRP
ジュルルッ
SHLURRP
ジュルルッ
AHNNNNN!
SQUIISH
ジュブッ
SHLURP
れろ
ジュブッ
SQUIISH
れろ
SHLURP
AHNNNNN!
SHPLOOSH
ブシュ
AGHNNN!
SHUDDER
ビクン

SHLIP
KWAAHHHHH!!!
SHLAP
AH!!
SHLAP
AH!!
AH!!
SHLAP
I'M HAPPY!! SO HAPPY!!
I WAITED... WAITED FOR SO LONG...!!
AHHHH!
AHHHH!

I MASTURBATED OVER AND OVER...
SHLLIP
AHH!
SO MANY DREAMS OF US MATING, YOTA...!!
SHPEWW
SHLLIP
AHH!
MY WHOLE BODY IS OVERFLOWING WITH HAPPINESS...
SHPEWW
OVERFLOWING WITH PLEASURE ...!
SHPEWW
SHPLURT
SHPLURT
I CAN'T THINK OF ANYTHING ELSE...!!
SHLAP
SHLAP
SHLAP
AH-HH-HH-HH-HH!

BUT... I DO KNOW ONE THING.
SOB
SOB
SOB
I'M GOING TO COOOOOME!!
I WAS... BORN TO MATE THIS DAY.
AHH!
AHH!
AGH-NN-NN-!!
SHOCK
SHOCK
SHOOOM
SHPLURRR...!
SHPLURRR...!
THUMP
THUMP

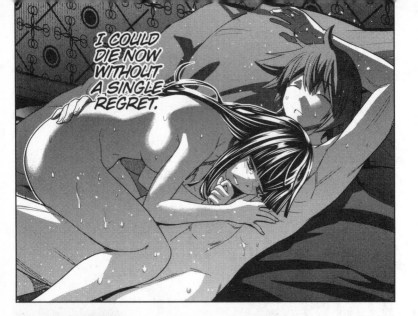

I COULD DIE NOW WITHOUT A SINGLE REGRET.

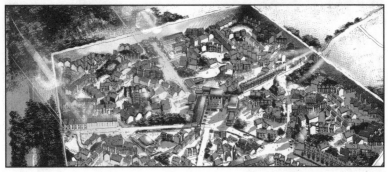

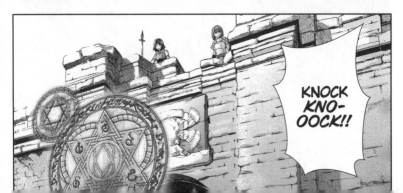

KNOCK KNO-OOCK!!

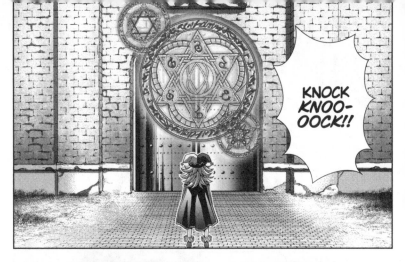

KNOCK KNOO-OOCK!!

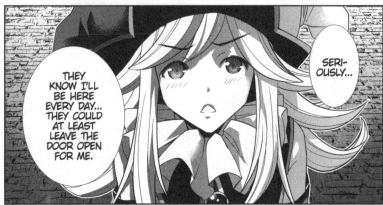

SERI-OUSLY...

THEY KNOW I'LL BE HERE EVERY DAY... THEY COULD AT LEAST LEAVE THE DOOR OPEN FOR ME.

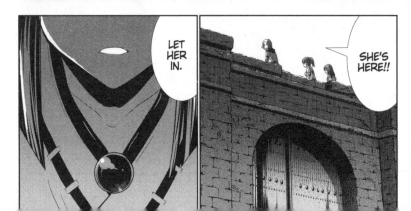

LET HER IN.

SHE'S HERE!!

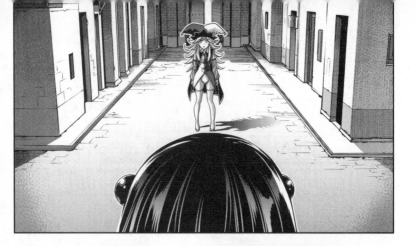

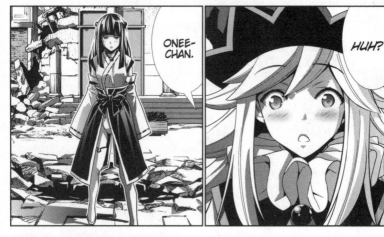

ONEE-
CHAN.

HUH?

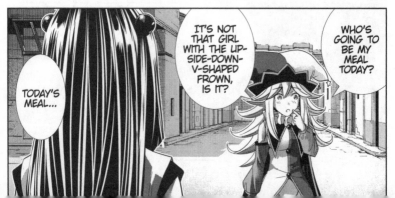

TODAY'S
MEAL...

IT'S NOT
THAT GIRL
WITH THE UP-
SIDE-DOWN-
V-SHAPED
FROWN,
IS IT?

WHO'S
GOING TO
BE MY
MEAL
TODAY?

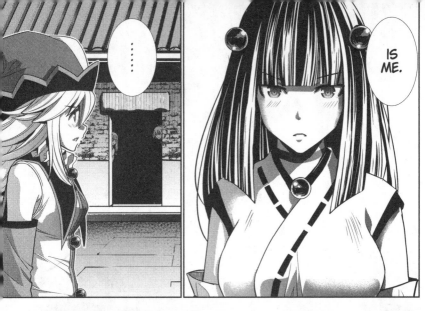

..... IS ME.

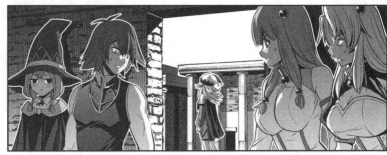

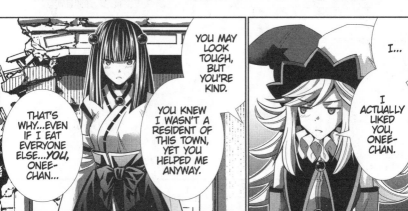

YOU MAY LOOK TOUGH, BUT YOU'RE KIND.

YOU KNEW I WASN'T A RESIDENT OF THIS TOWN, YET YOU HELPED ME ANYWAY.

THAT'S WHY...EVEN IF I EAT EVERYONE ELSE...*YOU,* ONEE-CHAN...

I...

I ACTUALLY LIKED YOU, ONEE-CHAN.

I WAS PLANNING ON EATING YOU LAST.
SO, YOU DID PLAN ON EATING ME.
BUT... I CAN'T LET MYSELF BE EATEN.
KA-SHHHNG
チャキーッ
SERI-OUSLY ...
UN-BELIEV-ABLE.

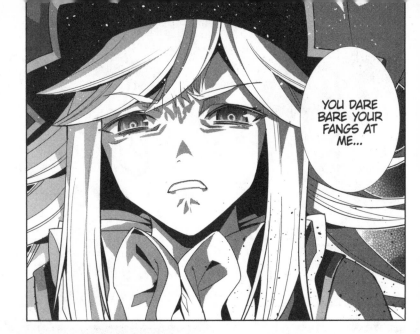

YOU DARE BARE YOUR FANGS AT ME...

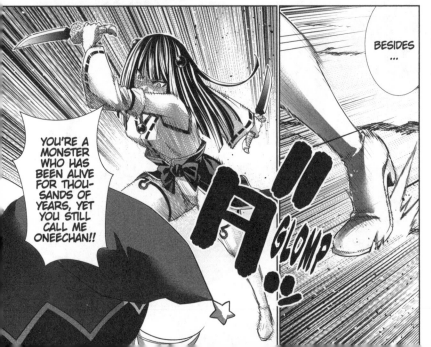

YOU'RE A MONSTER WHO HAS BEEN ALIVE FOR THOUSANDS OF YEARS, YET YOU STILL CALL ME ONEECHAN!!

BESIDES...

GLOMP

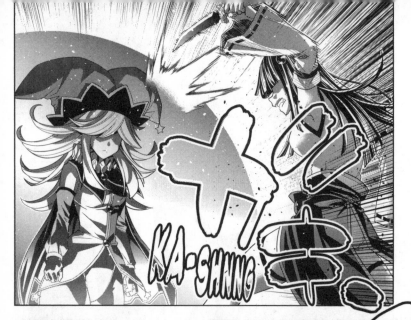

KA-SHHNG

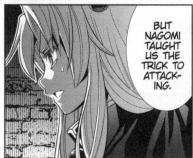

BUT NAGOMI TAUGHT US THE TRICK TO ATTACK-ING.

IT'S NO GOOD!!

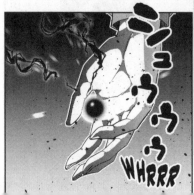

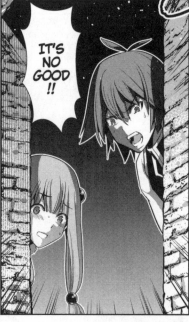

WHRRR

SHLIICE
WHAM
SHNNK

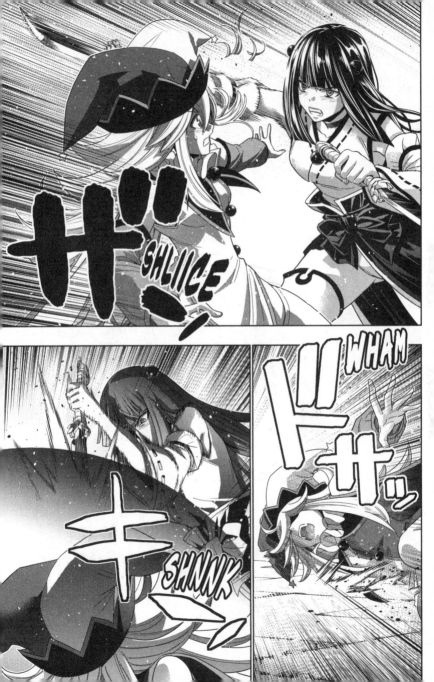

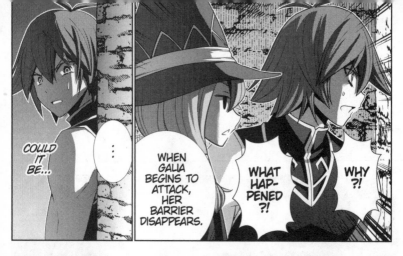

COULD IT BE...

:

WHEN GALIA BEGINS TO ATTACK, HER BARRIER DISAPPEARS.

WHAT HAP-PENED ?!

WHY ?!

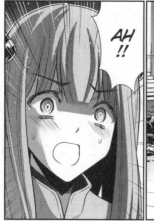

AH !!

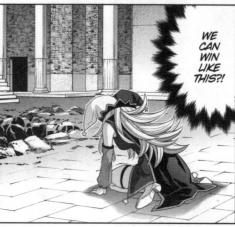

WE CAN WIN LIKE THIS?!

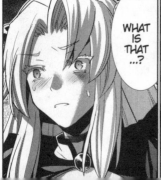

WHAT IS THAT ...?

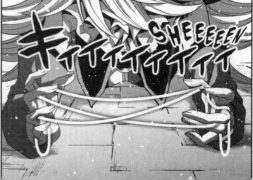

#ТТТТТТТТТТТ SHEEEEEN

...
YOU UNDER-ESTIMATE ME.
FYUUU
CHINCH
?!

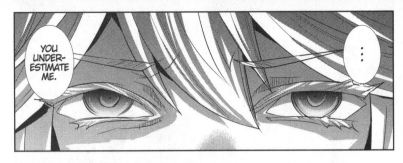

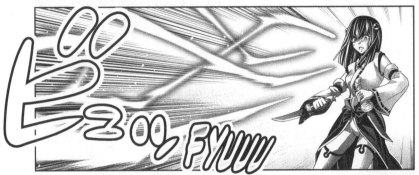

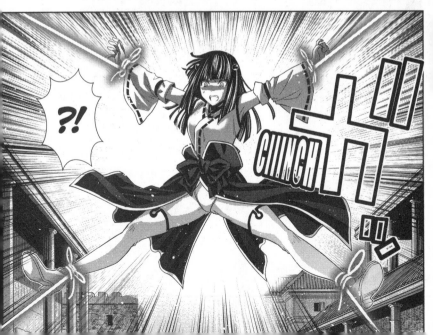

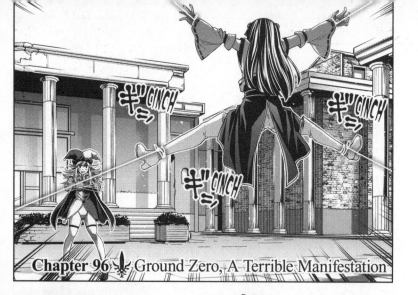

Chapter 96 ✦ Ground Zero, A Terrible Manifestation

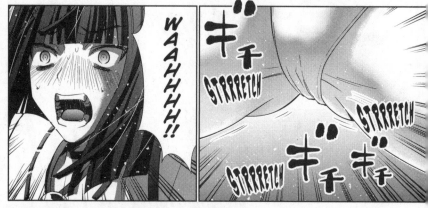

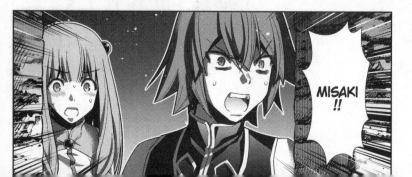

STAY AWAY!!
BYE BYE, ONEE-CHAN!!
CIIINCH
STRRRETCH
GAHHHHHH!!
STRRRETCH
STRRRETCH
THWWOOM

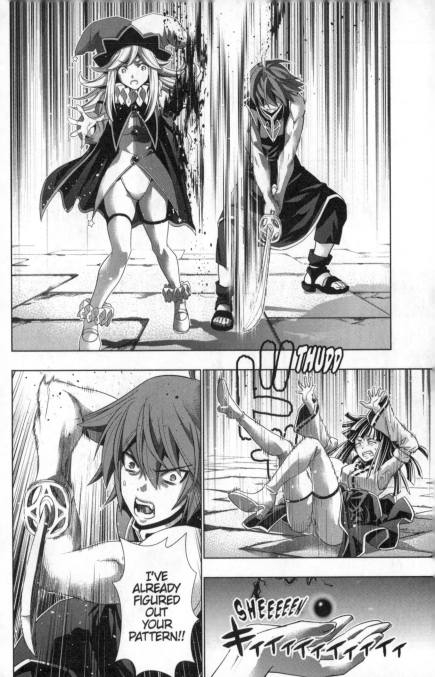

THUDD

I'VE ALREADY FIGURED OUT YOUR PATTERN!!

SHEEEEEN

ｷｨｨｨｨｨｨｨｨｨｨｨ

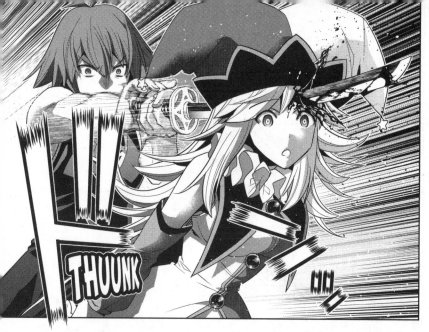

THUUNK

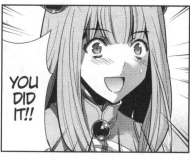

YOU DID IT!!

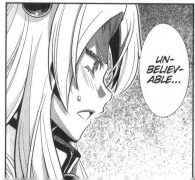

UN-BELIEV-ABLE...

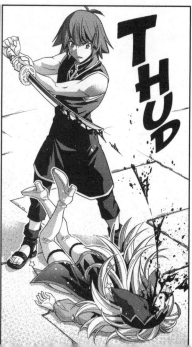

THUD

THE REAL BATTLE IS JUST BEGINNING.
SHLOP
ジュビ
SHLOP
ジュビ
SHLOP
ジュビ
SHLOP
ジュビ
SHLOP
ジュビ
SHLOP
ジュビ
SHLOP
ジュビ
SHLOP
ジュビ

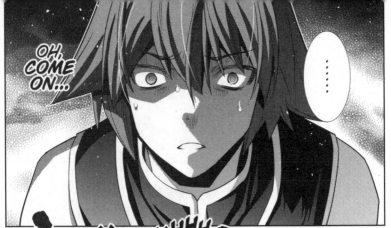

OH, COME ON...

. . . . .

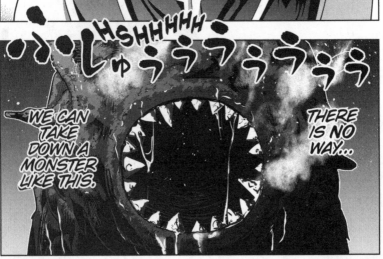

HSHHHHH

WE CAN TAKE DOWN A MONSTER LIKE THIS.

THERE IS NO WAY...

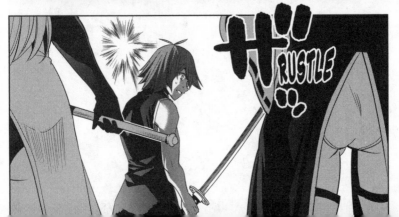

RUSTLE

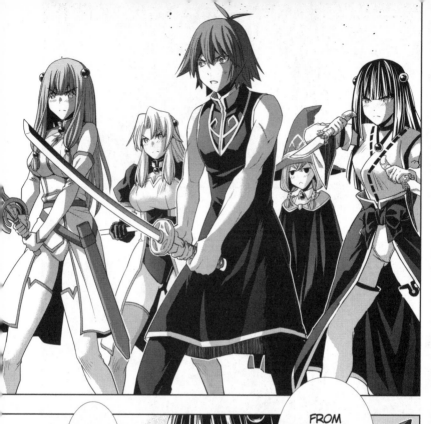

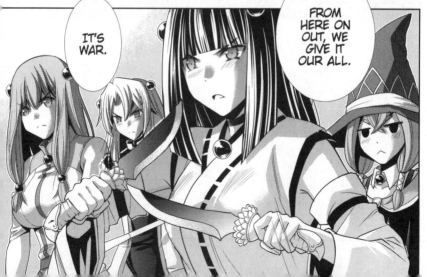

IT'S WAR.

FROM HERE ON OUT, WE GIVE IT OUR ALL.

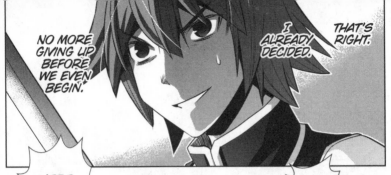

THAT'S RIGHT.

I ALREADY DECIDED.

NO MORE GIVING UP BEFORE WE EVEN BEGIN.

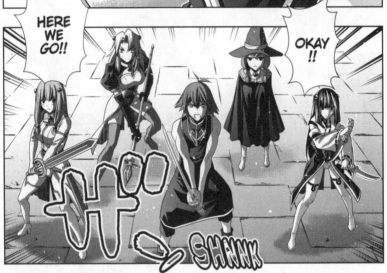

HERE WE GO!!

OKAY !!

SHNNK

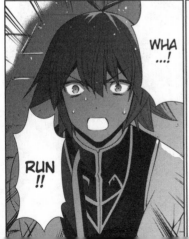

WHA ...!

RUN !!

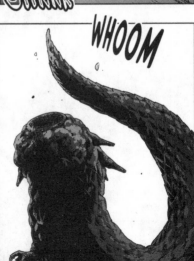

WHOOM

KA-WHOOM
GLOMP
YOU ...!!
SHAANG
SO HARD!!

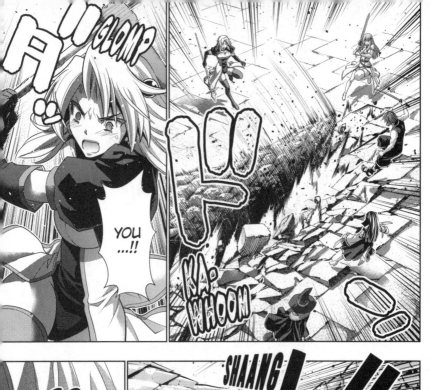

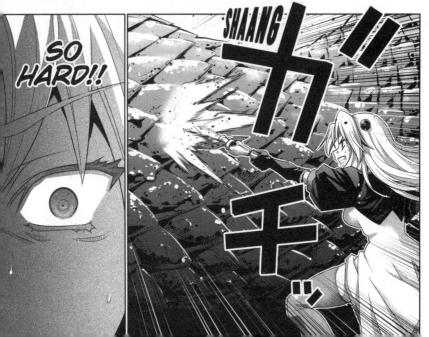

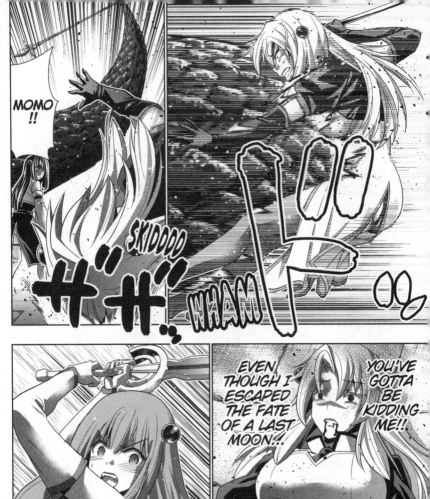

MOMO!!

SKIDDDD

WHAM

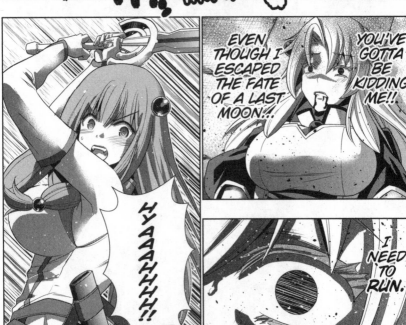

YOU'VE GOTTA BE KIDDING ME!!

EVEN THOUGH I ESCAPED THE FATE OF A LAST MOON!!..

HYAAAHHH!!

I NEED TO RUN.

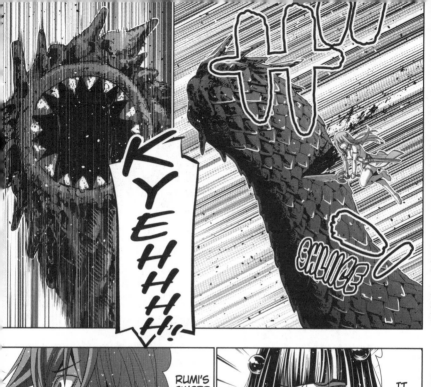

KYEHHHH!!

SHLICE

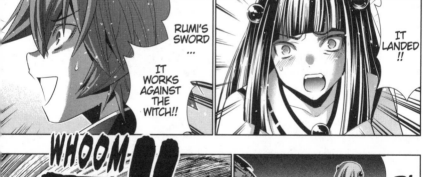

RUMI'S SWORD...

IT WORKS AGAINST THE WITCH!!

IT LANDED!!

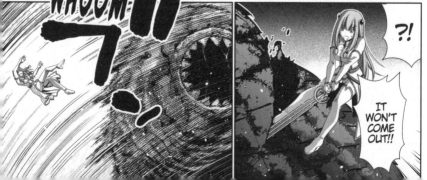

WHOOM!!

IT WON'T COME OUT!!

?!

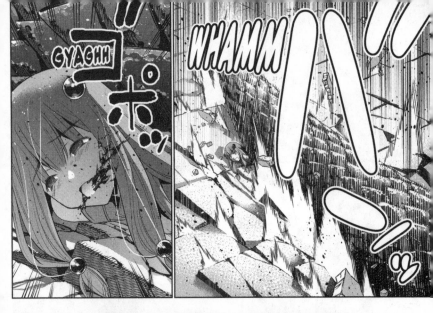

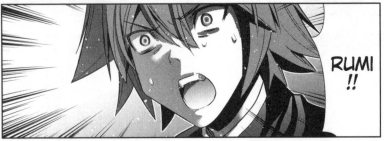

RUMI
!!

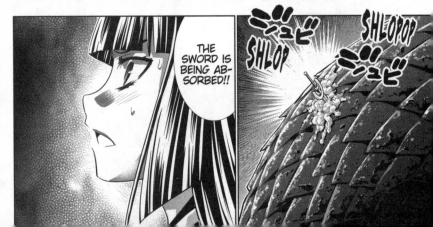

THE SWORD IS BEING ABSORBED!!

THUNK
THUNK
THNNK
CLUNK
CLUNK
KA-SHPLOOM

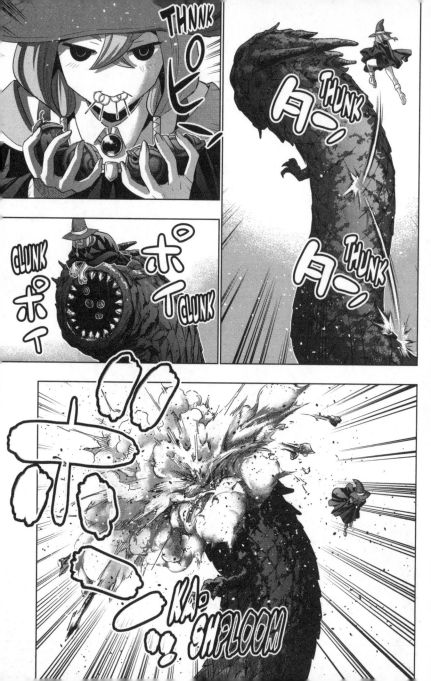

SHPLURRGE
DID SHE DO IT?!
CLENCH
?!
SHLOPOP
SHLOP
SHLOP

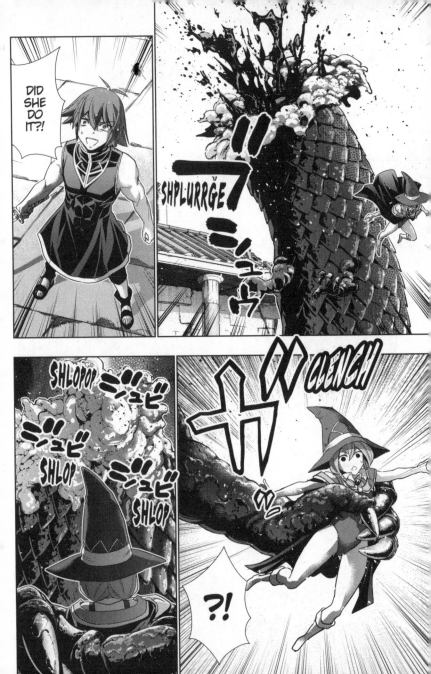

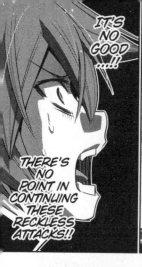

IT'S NO GOOD....!!

THERE'S NO POINT IN CONTINUING THESE RECKLESS ATTACKS!!

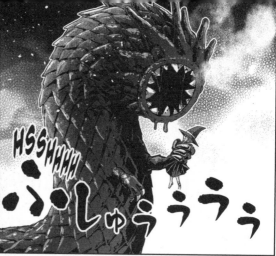

HSSHHHH

ふ‥しゅうぅぅぅ

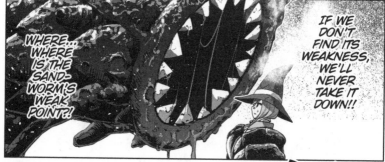

IF WE DON'T FIND ITS WEAKNESS, WE'LL NEVER TAKE IT DOWN!!

WHERE... WHERE IS THE SANDWORM'S WEAK POINT?!

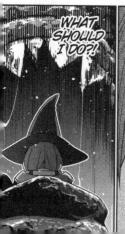

WHAT SHOULD I DO?!

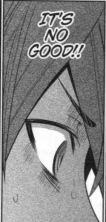

IT'S NO GOOD!!

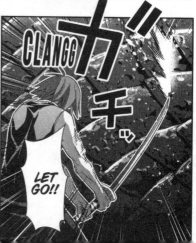

CLANGG ガ

チ

LET GO!!

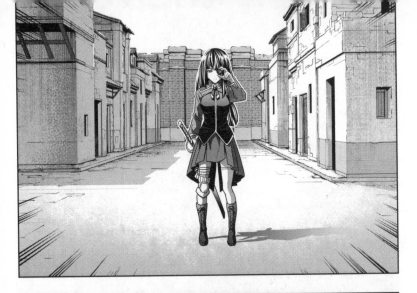

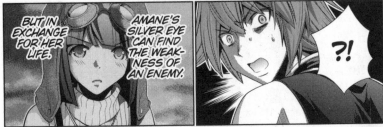

BUT IN EXCHANGE FOR HER LIFE.

AMANE'S SILVER EYE CAN FIND THE WEAKNESS OF AN ENEMY.

?!

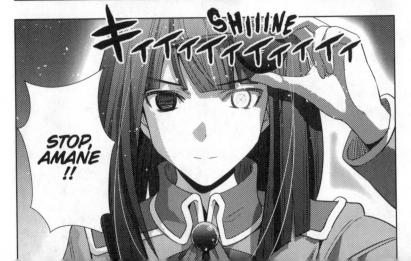

SHIIIINE

KIIIIIIIIIIIIII

STOP, AMANE!!

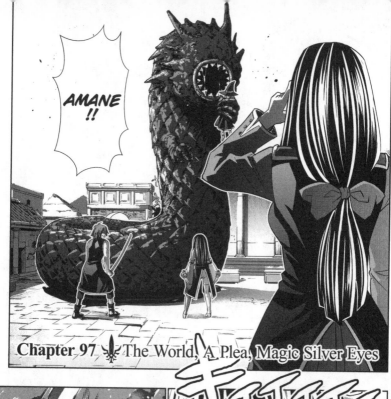

AMANE!!

Chapter 97 ❀ The World, A Plea, Magic Silver Eyes

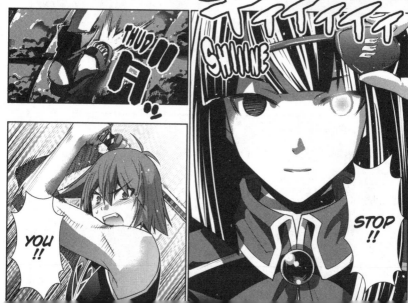

THUD!!

SHIIINE

YOU!!

STOP!!

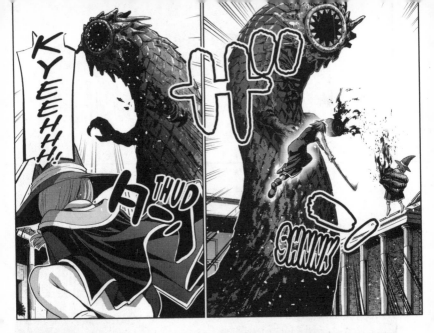

KYEEHHH!

THUD

SHNNK

AMANE!!

ITS ARM DOESN'T HAVE ANY SCALES AND CAN BE CUT!!

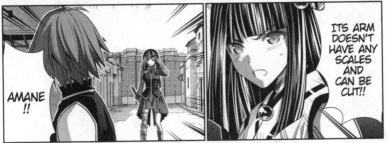

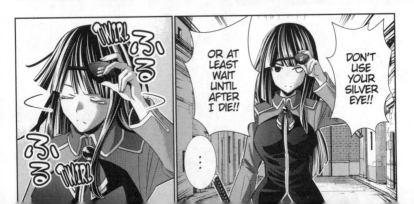

OR AT LEAST WAIT UNTIL AFTER I DIE!!

DON'T USE YOUR SILVER EYE!!

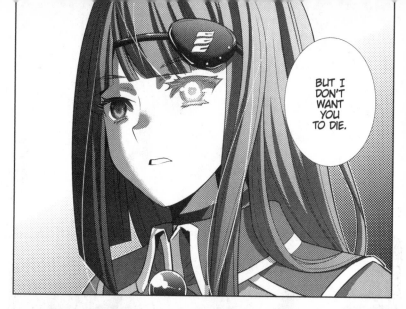

BUT I DON'T WANT YOU TO DIE.

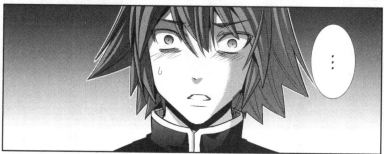

...

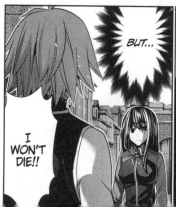

I WON'T DIE!!

BUT...

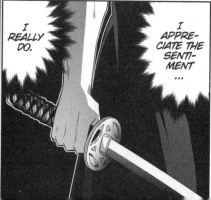

I REALLY DO.

I APPRE-CIATE THE SENTI-MENT...

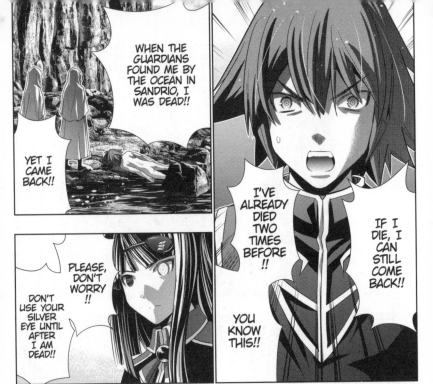

WHEN THE GUARDIANS FOUND ME BY THE OCEAN IN SANDRIO, I WAS DEAD!!

YET I CAME BACK!!

I'VE ALREADY DIED TWO TIMES BEFORE!!

IF I DIE, I CAN STILL COME BACK!!

YOU KNOW THIS!!

PLEASE, DON'T WORRY!!

DON'T USE YOUR SILVER EYE UNTIL AFTER I AM DEAD!!

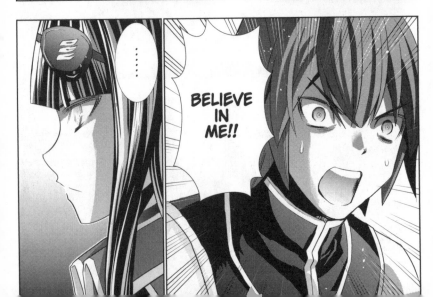

.....

BELIEVE IN ME!!

SHLIIP
スポッ

SHLOP
ジュビ
SHLOP
ジュビ

:

I'M SORRY, BUT THE CIRCUM- STANCES JUSTIFY A LIE.

ジュビ
SHLOP

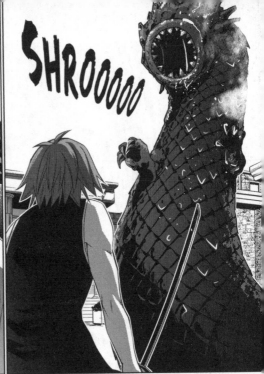

BUT... I STILL DON'T KNOW WHAT THE SANDWORM'S IS!!

THE MONSTERS IN THIS WORLD ALL HAVE A WEAKNESS!!

SHROOOOO

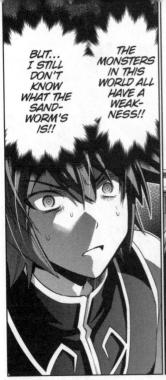

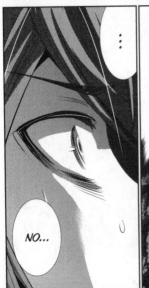

:

NO...

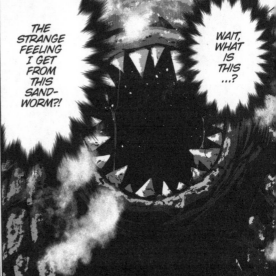

THE STRANGE FEELING I GET FROM THIS SANDWORM?!

WAIT, WHAT IS THIS...?

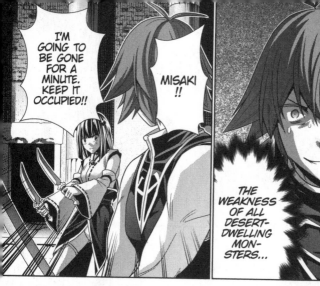

I'M GOING TO BE GONE FOR A MINUTE. KEEP IT OCCUPIED!!

MISAKI!!

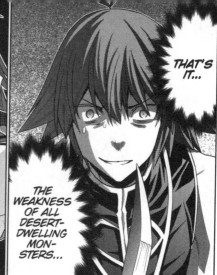

THAT'S IT...

THE WEAKNESS OF ALL DESERT-DWELLING MONSTERS...

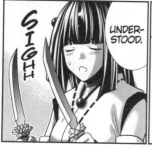

SIGHH

UNDERSTOOD.

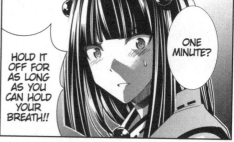

HOLD IT OFF FOR AS LONG AS YOU CAN HOLD YOUR BREATH!!

ONE MINUTE?

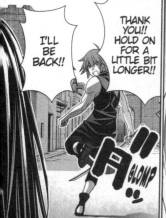

THANK YOU!! HOLD ON FOR A LITTLE BIT LONGER!!

I'LL BE BACK!!

GLOMP

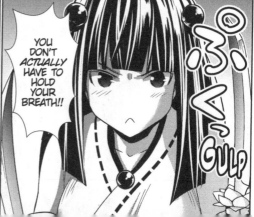

YOU DON'T ACTUALLY HAVE TO HOLD YOUR BREATH!!

GULP

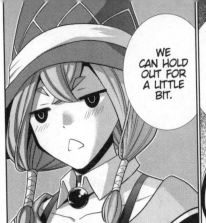

WE CAN HOLD OUT FOR A LITTLE BIT.

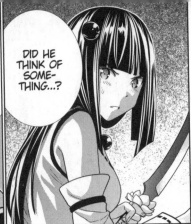

DID HE THINK OF SOMETHING...?

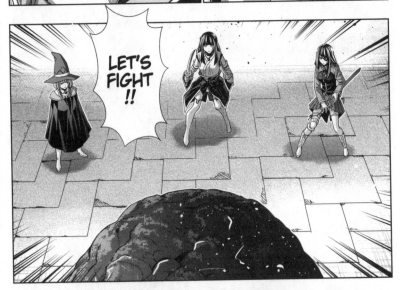

LET'S FIGHT!!

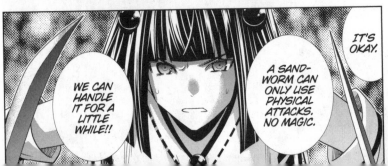

IT'S OKAY.

A SANDWORM CAN ONLY USE PHYSICAL ATTACKS. NO MAGIC.

WE CAN HANDLE IT FOR A LITTLE WHILE!!

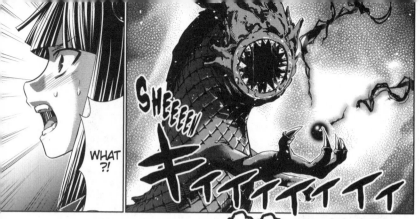

WHAT
?!

SHEEEEN

WHOOM

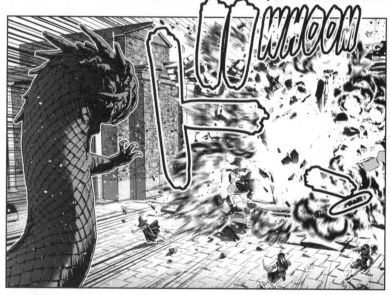

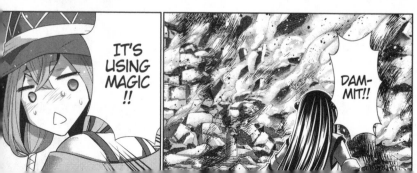

IT'S
USING
MAGIC
!!

DAM-
MIT!!

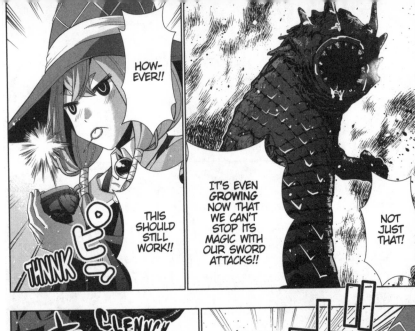

HOW-
EVER!!

THIS
SHOULD
STILL
WORK!!

THNNK

IT'S EVEN
GROWING
NOW THAT
WE CAN'T
STOP ITS
MAGIC WITH
OUR SWORD
ATTACKS!!

NOT
JUST
THAT!

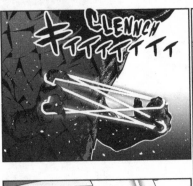

CLENNCH

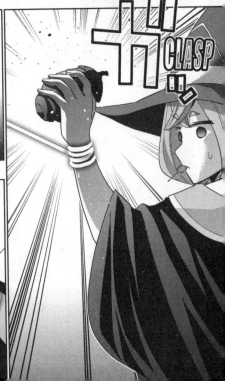

CLASP

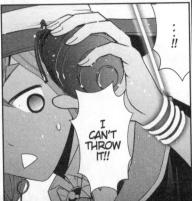

...!!

I
CAN'T
THROW
IT!!

KA-WHOOM
THUNK
KIA !!
SKKIIID

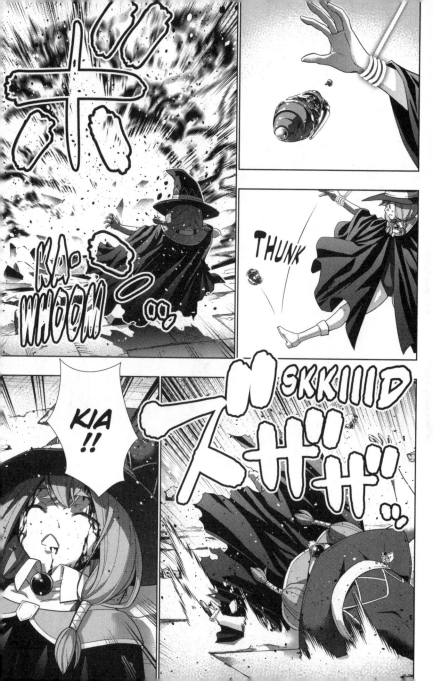

オオオ
オオオ
WHOOOOOM
?!
IT'S HUGE !!
SCCRAPE
ズズッ
RUN !!

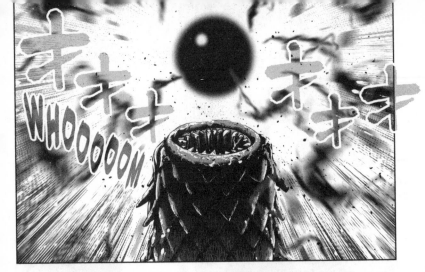

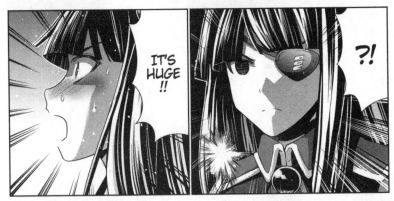

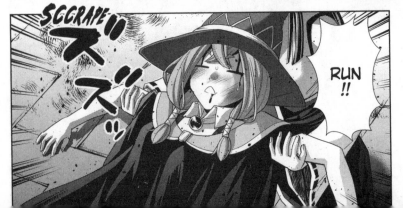

UNTIL YOTA ...!!
UNTIL YOTA RETURNS ...!!
KA-SPLASH
KA-
SPLASH
IT'S WATER!! IT HAS TO BE!!
WATER IS A WEAKNESS FOR MON-STERS WHO LIVE WHERE THERE IS NONE. IT'S PERFECT!!

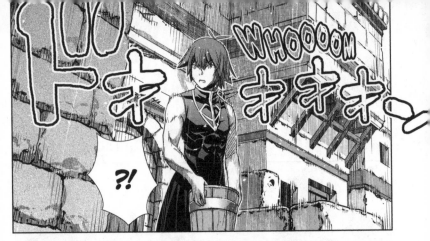

?!

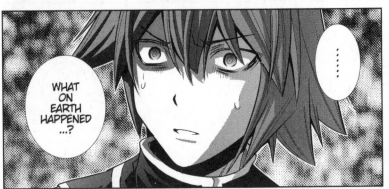

WHAT ON EARTH HAPPENED ...?

......

?!

THUD

THUD

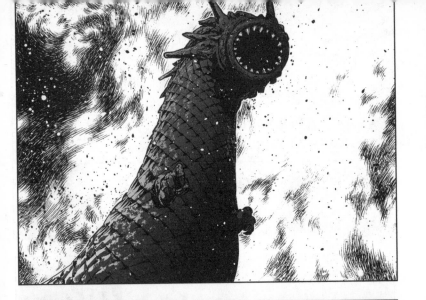

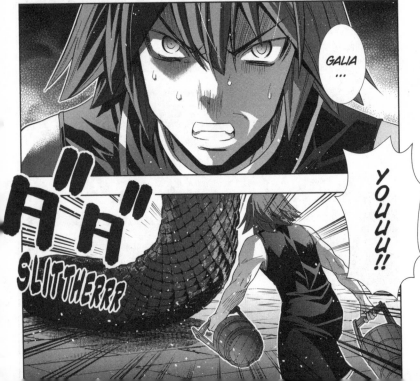

GALIA
...

YOUUUU!!

"ЯЯ"
SLITTHERRR

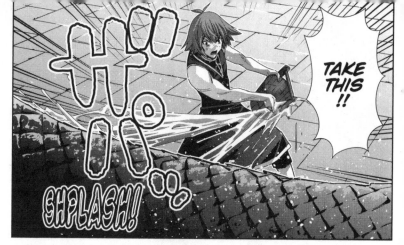

TAKE THIS !!

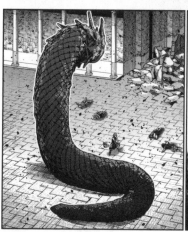

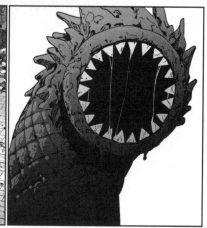

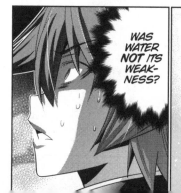

WAS WATER NOT ITS WEAKNESS?

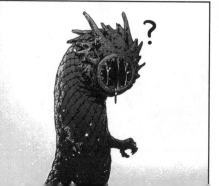

WHRRRRRRR
......
IT'S NO...
USE...
OOOOOOO
NO!!

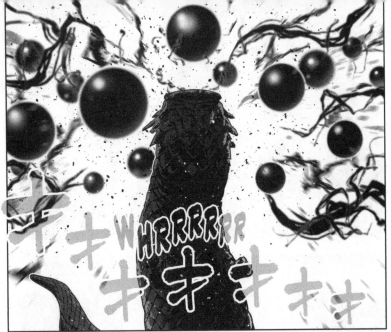

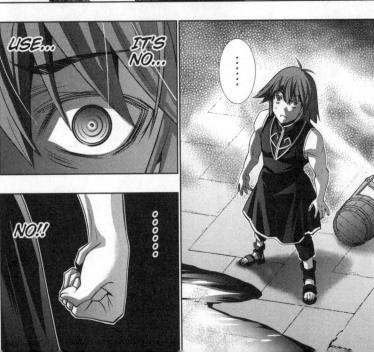

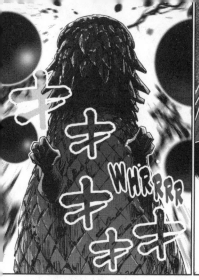

キ キ キ
WHIRRRR
キ キ

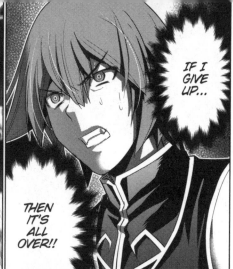

IF I GIVE UP...

THEN IT'S ALL OVER!!

HUH ?!

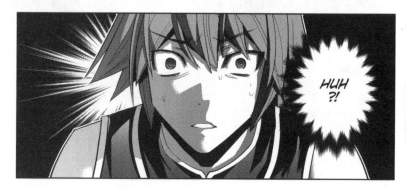

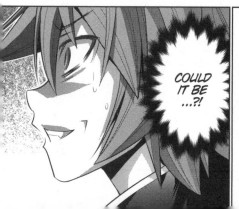

COULD IT BE ...?!

THE ONE I FELT BEFORE...

THAT STRANGE FEELING...

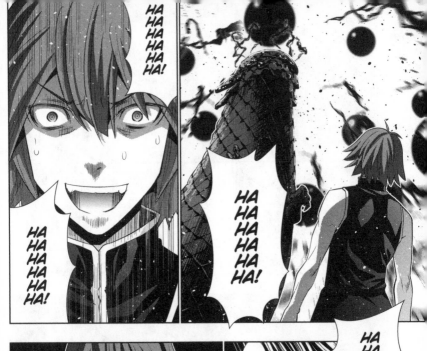

HA HA HA HA HA!

HA HA HA HA HA HA!

HA HA HA HA HA HA!

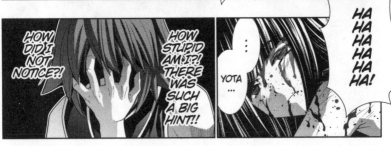

HOW DID I NOT NOTICE?!

HOW STUPID AM I?! THERE WAS SUCH A BIG HINT!!

... YOTA...

HA HA HA HA HA HA!

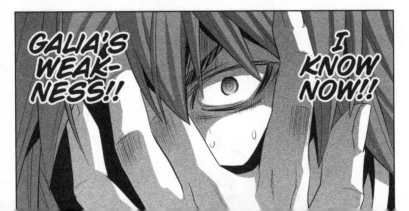

GALIA'S WEAKNESS!!

I KNOW NOW!!

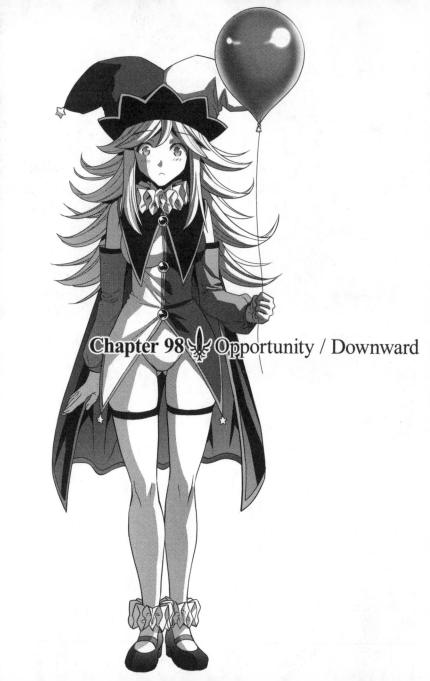

Chapter 98 Opportunity / Downward

HA HA HA HA HA HA!
HA HA HA HA HA HA!
I GOT IT!!
I FINALLY GOT IT!! ITS WEAK- NESS!!

WHRR
...
IT'S SO HUGE ...
ビュオオオオオオ
WHROOOOON
IT'S PLANNING... ON TAKING OUT THIS WHOLE TOWN...

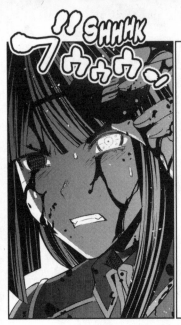

SHHHK

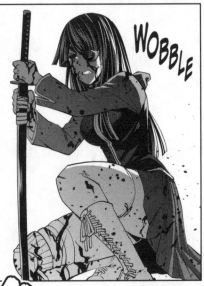

WOBBLE

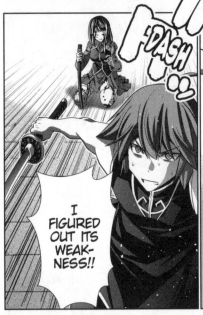

F'DASH!!

I FIGURED OUT ITS WEAKNESS!!

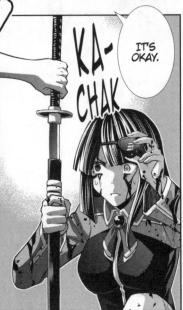

KA-CHAK

IT'S OKAY.

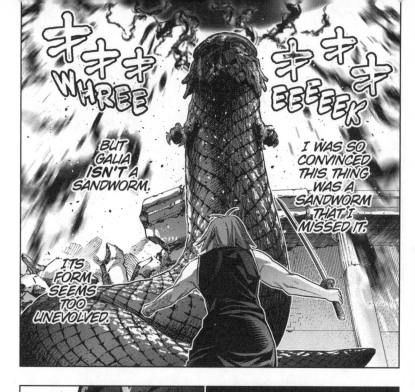

BUT GALIA ISN'T A SANDWORM.

ITS FORM SEEMS TOO UNEVOLVED.

I WAS SO CONVINCED THIS THING WAS A SANDWORM THAT I MISSED IT.

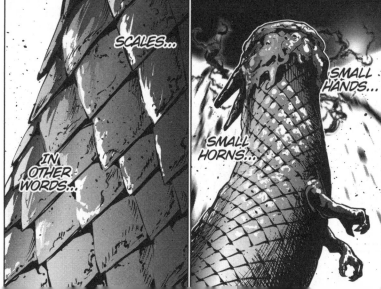

SCALES...

IN OTHER WORDS...

SMALL HORNS...

SMALL HANDS...

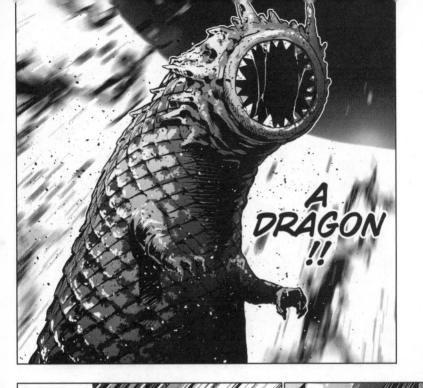

A DRAGON!!

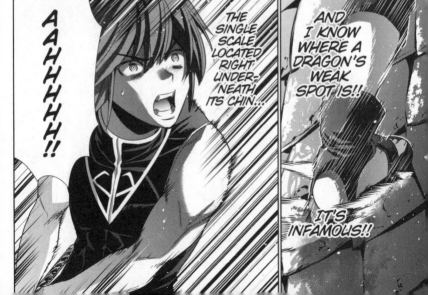

AAHHHHH!!

THE SINGLE SCALE LOCATED RIGHT UNDERNEATH ITS CHIN...

AND I KNOW WHERE A DRAGON'S WEAK SPOT IS!!

IT'S INFAMOUS!!

WHOOM
THE DRAGON'S WRATH!!

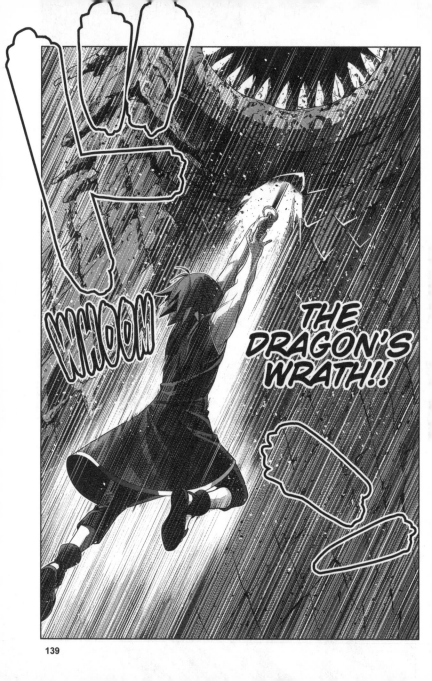

THUD

?
NO WAY...
I WAS WRONG AGAIN?!
THERE IS NO...
STOPPING IT NOW.

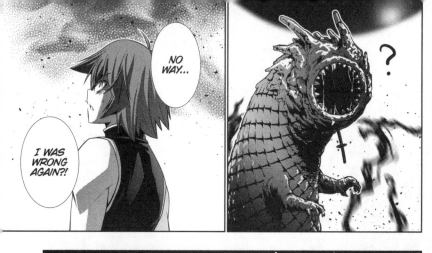

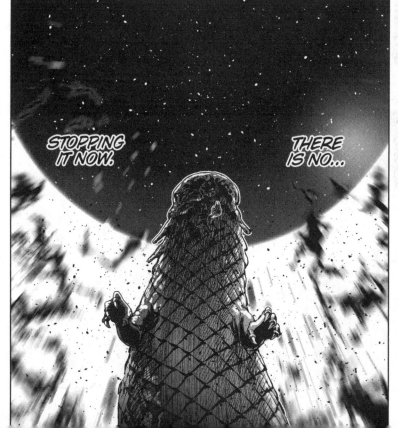

SHOOM
?!
KIEEEEE!

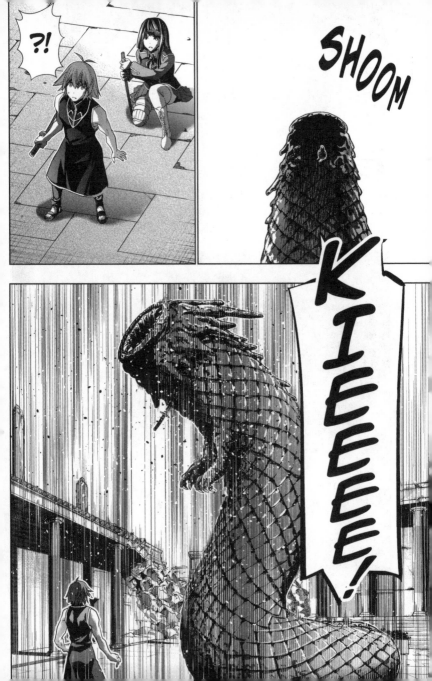

KIIEEEEEE!
ドロ
SHLOP
ドロ
SHLOP
GOAAAAA!
ドロ
SHLOP
GAAAAAAA!
ドロドロ
SHLOPOP
SHLOP
ブシュウ
SHPLURRGE

しゅううううううう
FSSSSKKKK
AH...
AHH...

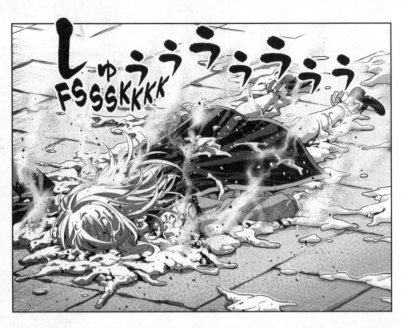

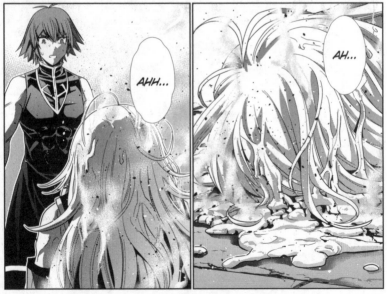

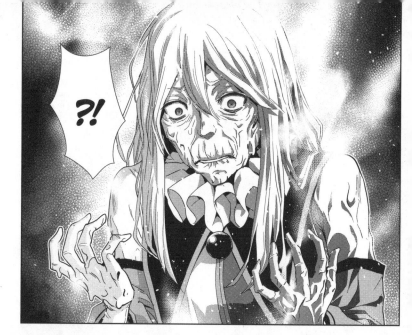

?!

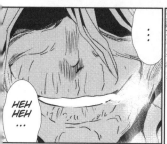

:

HEH
HEH
...

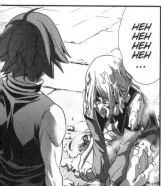

HEH
HEH
HEH
HEH
...

THOUGH,
YOU LOOK
YOUNG
FOR YOUR
AGE.

WELL,
YOU ARE
OVER
THREE
THOU-
SAND
YEARS
OLD.

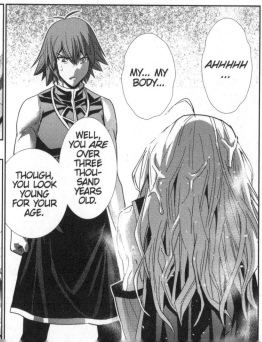

MY... MY
BODY...

AHHHHH
...

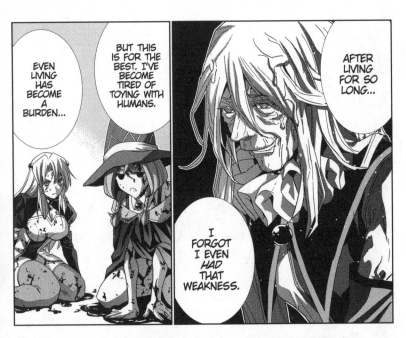

EVEN LIVING HAS BECOME A BURDEN...

BUT THIS IS FOR THE BEST. I'VE BECOME TIRED OF TOYING WITH HUMANS.

AFTER LIVING FOR SO LONG...

I FORGOT I EVEN *HAD* THAT WEAKNESS.

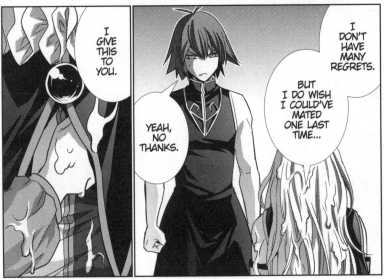

I GIVE THIS TO YOU.

YEAH, NO THANKS.

I DON'T HAVE MANY REGRETS.

BUT I DO WISH I COULD'VE MATED ONE LAST TIME...

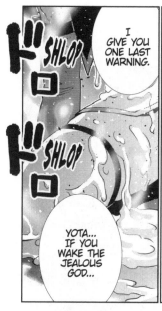

I GIVE YOU ONE LAST WARNING.

YOTA... IF YOU WAKE THE JEALOUS GOD...

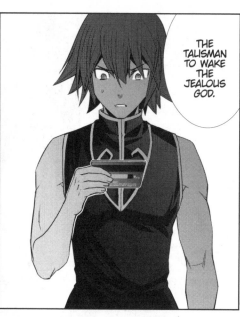

THE TALISMAN TO WAKE THE JEALOUS GOD.

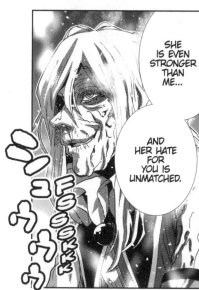

SHE IS EVEN STRONGER THAN ME...

AND HER HATE FOR YOU IS UNMATCHED.

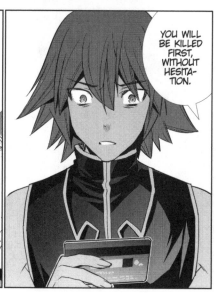

YOU WILL BE KILLED FIRST, WITHOUT HESITATION.

...
I DON'T DOUBT IT.
SHLOP SHLOP
I'M TIRED ...
SO TIRED ...
DRIBBLE
DRIBBLE
TIRED...
FSSKKKK
GOOD NIGHT ...
SHPLOOSH

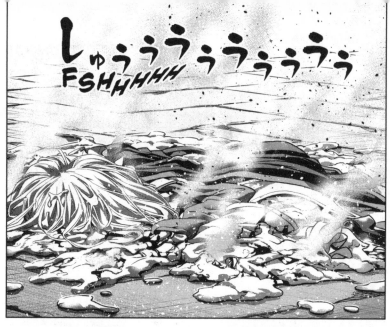

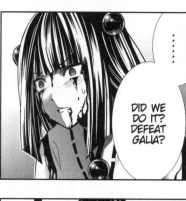

DID WE DO IT? DEFEAT GALIA?

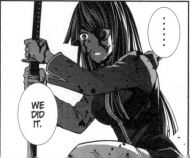

WE DID IT.

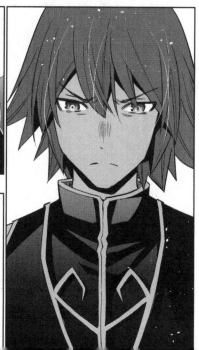

WOOHOO!
YAYY!

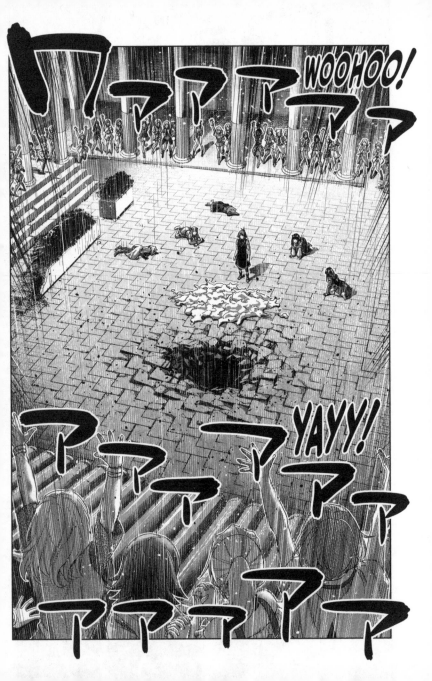

WOOOOO!
......
DID YOU DEFEAT GALIA?
WOOHOO!
HM?

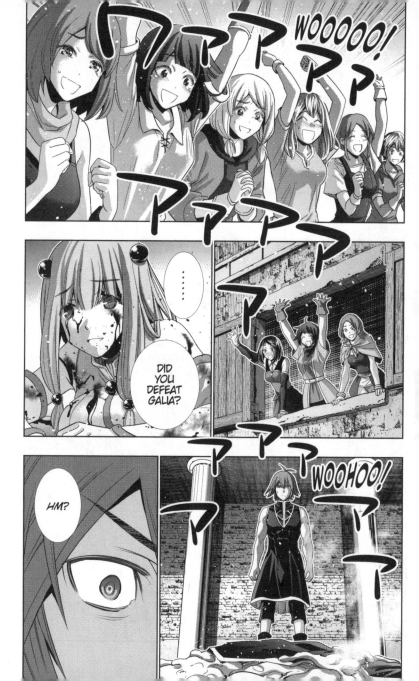

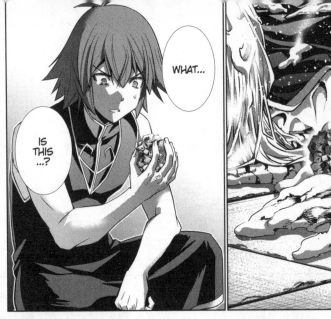

WHAT...

IS THIS ...?

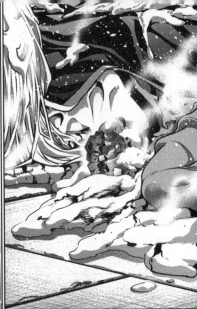

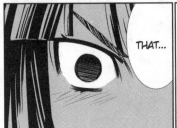

THAT...

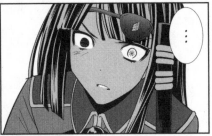

...

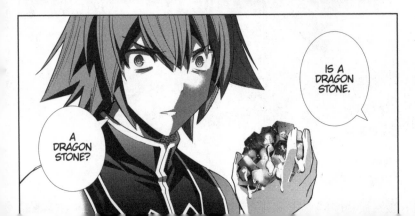

IS A DRAGON STONE.

A DRAGON STONE?

Chapter 99 HURT THE HEART

I THINK THAT COULD BE...
A DRAGON STONE.
A DRAGON STONE ...?
IT IS AN INVALUABLE SOURCE OF MATERIAL FOR CREATING WEAPONS.
IT CAN ONLY BE FOUND WITHIN DRAGONS.

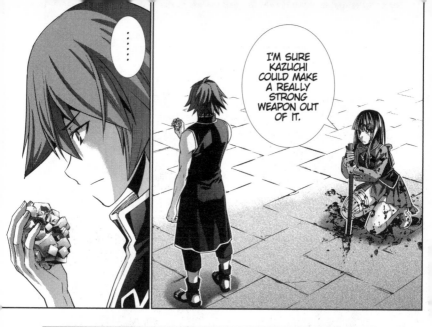

. . . . . .

I'M SURE KAZUCHI COULD MAKE A REALLY STRONG WEAPON OUT OF IT.

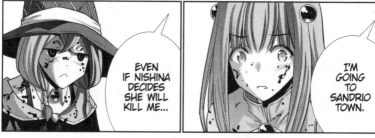

EVEN IF NISHINA DECIDES SHE WILL KILL ME...

I'M GOING TO SANDRIO TOWN.

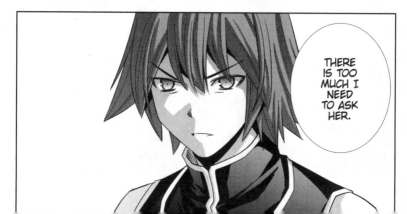

THERE IS TOO MUCH I NEED TO ASK HER.

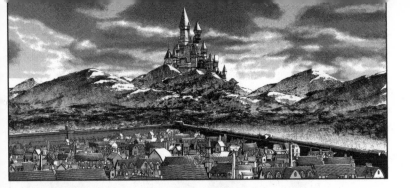

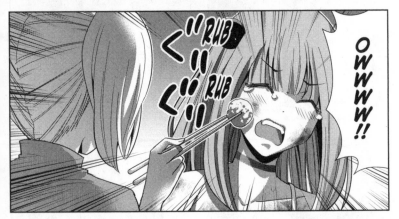

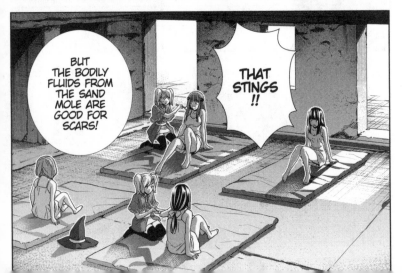

BUT THE BODILY FLUIDS FROM THE SAND MOLE ARE GOOD FOR SCARS!

THAT STINGS!!

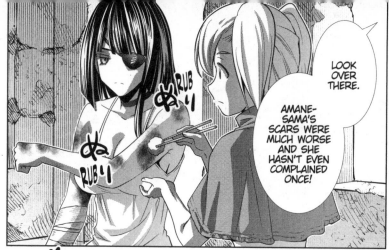

LOOK OVER THERE.

AMANE-SAMA'S SCARS WERE MUCH WORSE AND SHE HASN'T EVEN COMPLAINED ONCE!

RUB ♪

RUB ♪

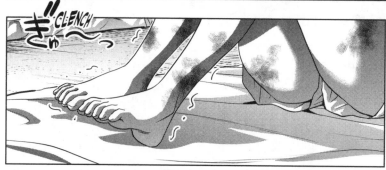

CLENCH

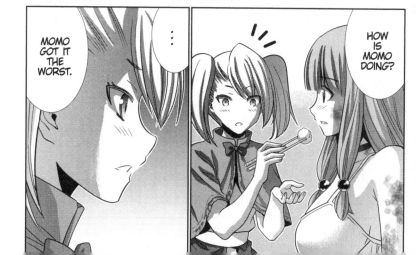

MOMO GOT IT THE WORST.

...

HOW IS MOMO DOING?

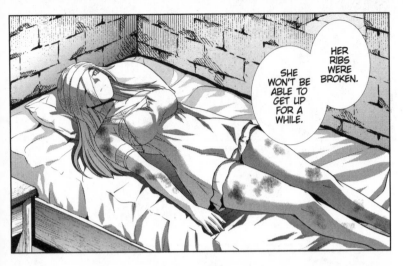

HER RIBS WERE BROKEN.

SHE WON'T BE ABLE TO GET UP FOR A WHILE.

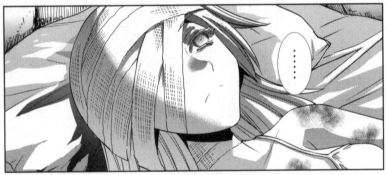

. . . . .

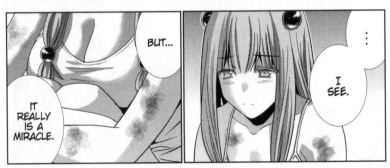

BUT...

IT REALLY IS A MIRACLE.

:

I SEE.

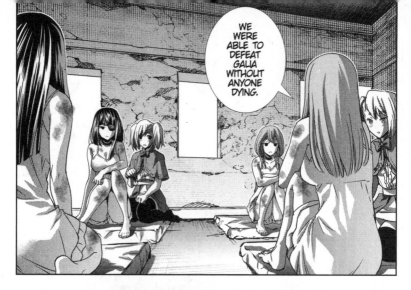

WE WERE ABLE TO DEFEAT GALIA WITHOUT ANYONE DYING.

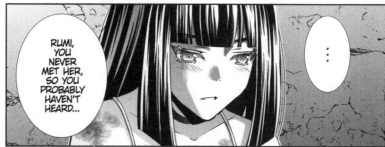

RUMI, YOU NEVER MET HER, SO YOU PROBABLY HAVEN'T HEARD...

...

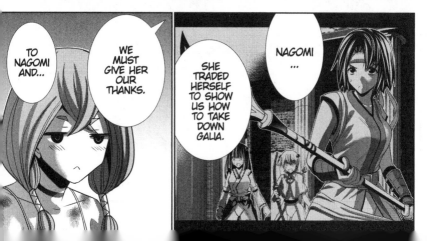

TO NAGOMI AND...

WE MUST GIVE HER OUR THANKS.

SHE TRADED HERSELF TO SHOW US HOW TO TAKE DOWN GALIA.

NAGOMI
...

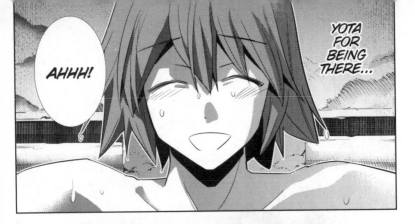

YOTA FOR BEING THERE...

AHHH!

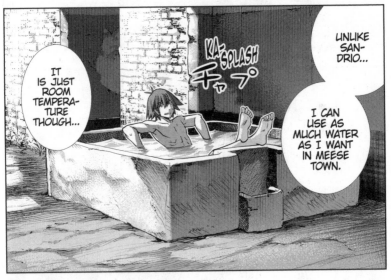

IT IS JUST ROOM TEMPERATURE THOUGH...

KA SPLASH
チ ャ プ

UNLIKE SANDRIO...

I CAN USE AS MUCH WATER AS I WANT IN MEESE TOWN.

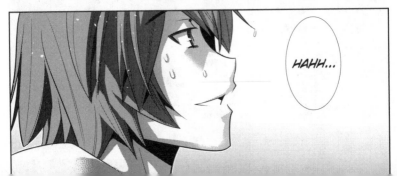

HAHH...

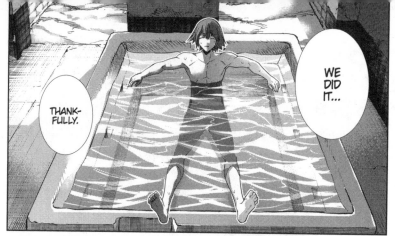

WE DID IT...

THANK-FULLY.

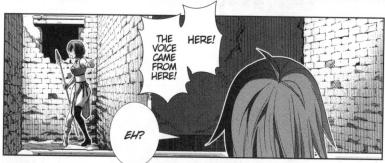

THE VOICE CAME FROM HERE!

HERE!

EH?

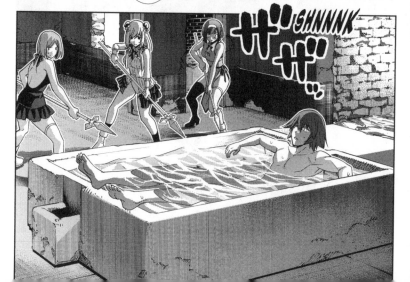

H' GHNNNK

HF'

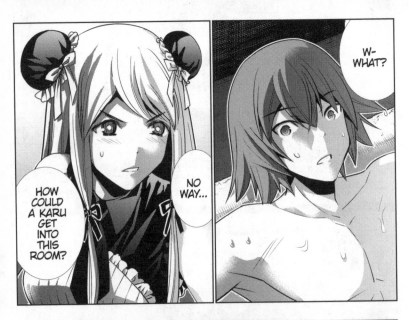

HOW COULD A KARU GET INTO THIS ROOM?

NO WAY...

W-WHAT?

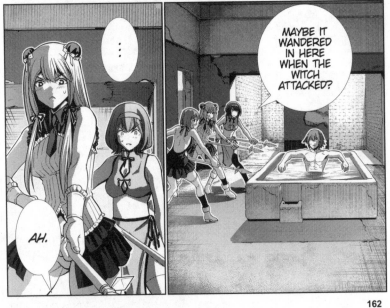

...

AH.

MAYBE IT WANDERED IN HERE WHEN THE WITCH ATTACKED?

YOU CAUGHT ME OFF GUARD. I FORGOT TO EAT THE CANDY.
THE RESIDENTS OF MEESE TOWN WILL FIGURE OUT WHO I AM FROM MY VOICE.
?!
THE KARU !!
IT SPOKE !!
A NEW TYPE ?!
I'M NOT A KARU.
PUT YOUR HANDS UP AND STAND!!
EH...
BUT I'M COMPLETELY NAKED...
KARU ARE ALWAYS NAKED!!
STAND !!

KA-SPLASH
......
......

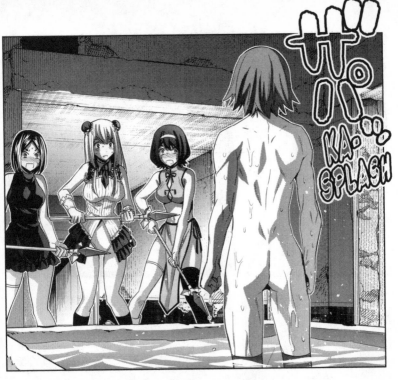

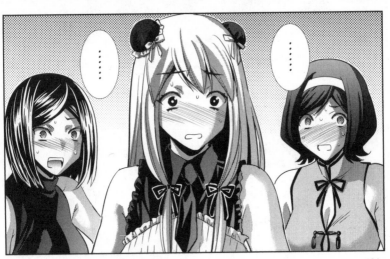

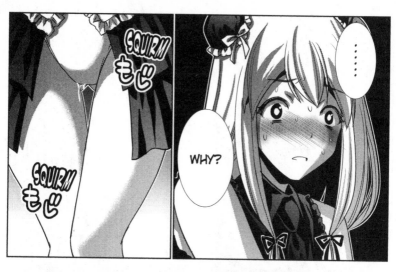

SQUIRM
もじ

SQUIRM
もじ

・・・・・

WHY?

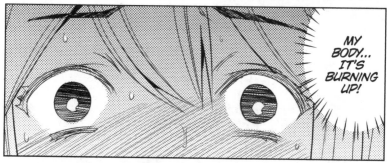

MY BODY... IT'S BURNING UP!

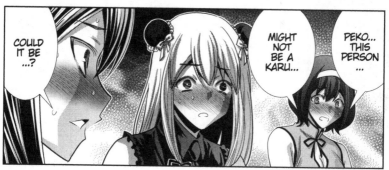

COULD IT BE ...?

MIGHT NOT BE A KARU...

PEKO... THIS PERSON ...

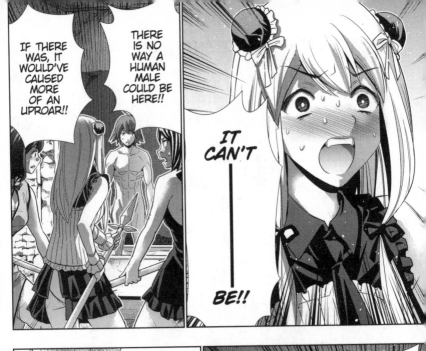

IF THERE WAS, IT WOULD'VE CAUSED MORE OF AN UPROAR!!

THERE IS NO WAY A HUMAN MALE COULD BE HERE!!

IT CAN'T

BE!!

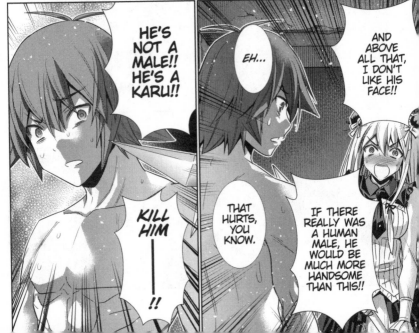

HE'S NOT A MALE!! HE'S A KARU!!

KILL HIM

!!

EH...

THAT HURTS, YOU KNOW.

AND ABOVE ALL THAT, I DON'T LIKE HIS FACE!!

IF THERE REALLY WAS A HUMAN MALE, HE WOULD BE MUCH MORE HANDSOME THAN THIS!!

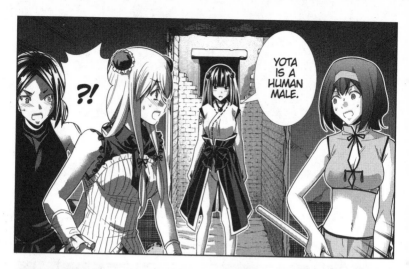

?!

YOTA IS A HUMAN MALE.

I WAS AFRAID TELLING YOU WOULD START A PANIC.

I'M SORRY FOR HIDING IT FROM YOU.

MISAKI-SAMA!

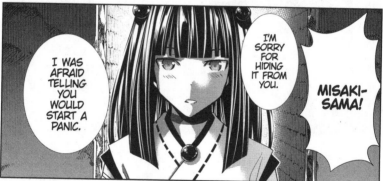

BUT YOTA IS THE HERO WHO DEFEATED GALIA AND SAVED THE TOWN.

YOU THREE HAD EVACUATED, SO YOU PROBABLY DIDN'T SEE...

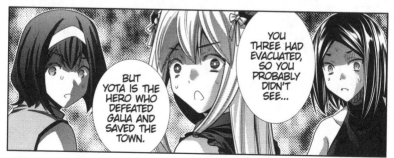

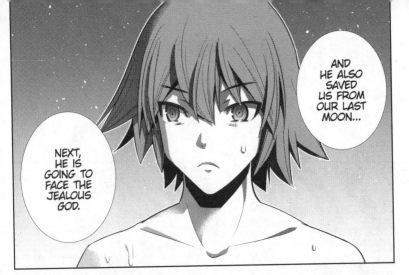

AND HE ALSO SAVED US FROM OUR LAST MOON...

NEXT, HE IS GOING TO FACE THE JEALOUS GOD.

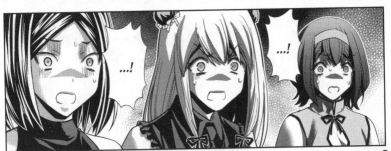

...!

...!

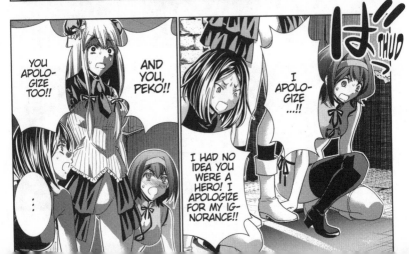

YOU APOLO-GIZE TOO!!

AND YOU, PEKO!!

...

I APOLO-GIZE...!!

I HAD NO IDEA YOU WERE A HERO! I APOLOGIZE FOR MY IG-NORANCE!!

THUD

I'LL NEVER ACCEPT THAT *THING* AS A HUMAN MALE!!

I'M HALLUCI-NATING!! HALLUCI-NATING!!

NEVERRR!!

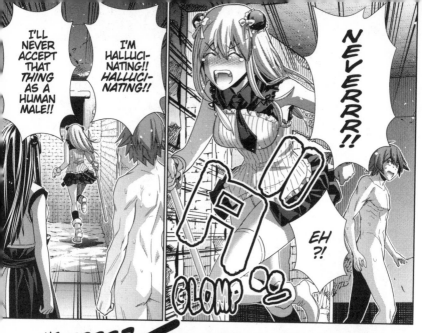

GLOMP

EH ?!

NEVERRRR

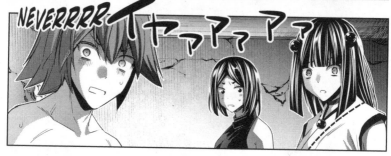

THAT ...

THAT ACTUALLY HURT A BIT...

:

I'M SORRY.

PEKO IS JUST AS GOOD AS ANY GUARDIAN WITH WEAPONS, BUT SHE HAS A MOUTH.

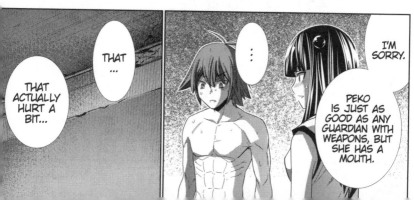

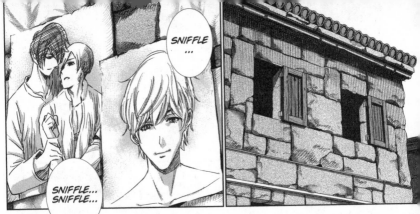

SNIFFLE...

SNIFFLE... SNIFFLE...

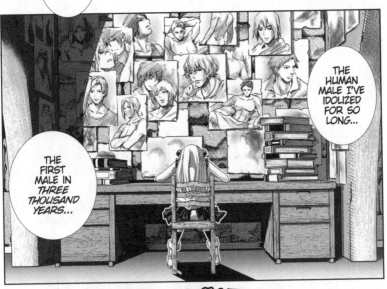

THE HUMAN MALE I'VE IDOLIZED FOR SO LONG...

THE FIRST MALE IN *THREE THOUSAND YEARS*...

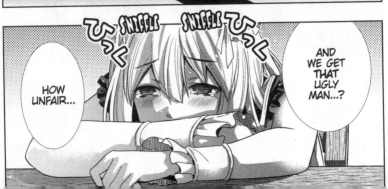

HOW UNFAIR...

AND WE GET THAT UGLY MAN...?

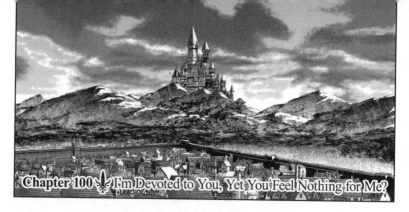

Chapter 100 ⚜ I'm Devoted to You, Yet You Feel Nothing for Me?

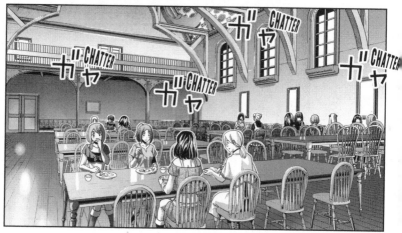

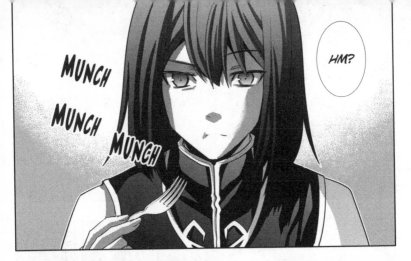

MUNCH

MUNCH

MUNCH

HM?

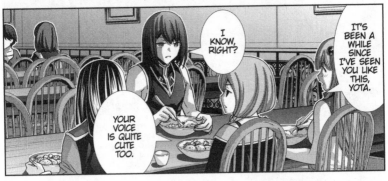

IT'S BEEN A WHILE SINCE I'VE SEEN YOU LIKE THIS, YOTA.

I KNOW?

YOUR VOICE IS QUITE CUTE TOO.

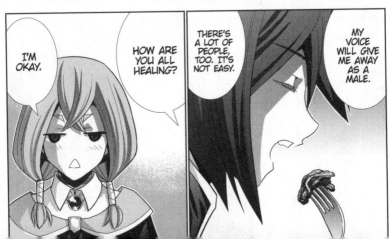

MY VOICE WILL GIVE ME AWAY AS A MALE.

THERE'S A LOT OF PEOPLE, TOO. IT'S NOT EASY.

HOW ARE YOU ALL HEALING?

I'M OKAY.

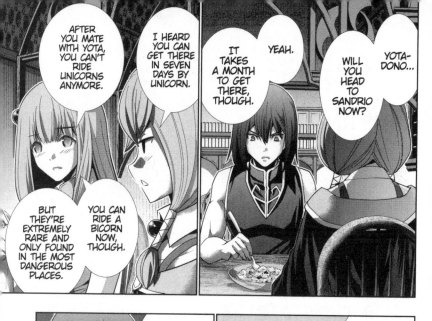

AFTER YOU MATE WITH YOTA, YOU CAN'T RIDE UNICORNS ANYMORE.

I HEARD YOU CAN GET THERE IN SEVEN DAYS BY UNICORN.

IT TAKES A MONTH TO GET THERE, THOUGH.

YEAH.

WILL YOU HEAD TO SANDRIO NOW?

YOTA-DONO...

BUT THEY'RE EXTREMELY RARE AND ONLY FOUND IN THE MOST DANGEROUS PLACES.

YOU CAN RIDE A BICORN NOW, THOUGH.

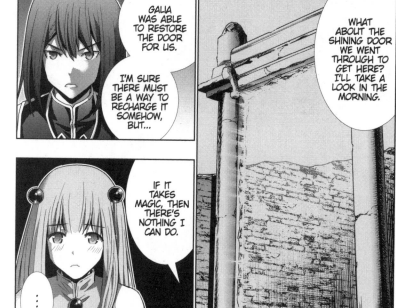

GALIA WAS ABLE TO RESTORE THE DOOR FOR US.

I'M SURE THERE MUST BE A WAY TO RECHARGE IT SOMEHOW, BUT...

WHAT ABOUT THE SHINING DOOR WE WENT THROUGH TO GET HERE? I'LL TAKE A LOOK IN THE MORNING.

IF IT TAKES MAGIC, THEN THERE'S NOTHING I CAN DO.

...

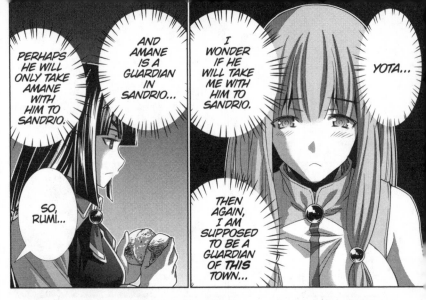

PERHAPS HE WILL ONLY TAKE AMANE WITH HIM TO SANDRIO.

AND AMANE IS A GUARDIAN IN SANDRIO...

I WONDER IF HE WILL TAKE ME WITH HIM TO SANDRIO.

YOTA...

SO, RUMI...

THEN AGAIN, I AM SUPPOSED TO BE A GUARDIAN OF THIS TOWN...

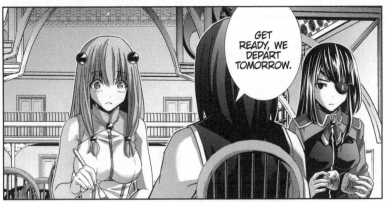

GET READY, WE DEPART TOMORROW.

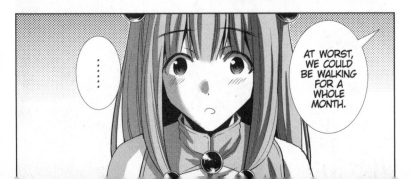

. . . .

AT WORST, WE COULD BE WALKING FOR A WHOLE MONTH.

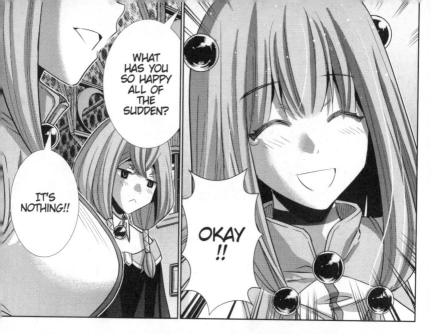

WHAT HAS YOU SO HAPPY ALL OF THE SUDDEN?

IT'S NOTHING!!

OKAY!!

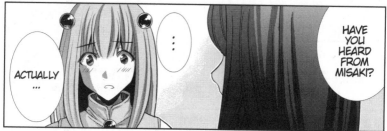

HAVE YOU HEARD FROM MISAKI?

ACTUALLY...

...

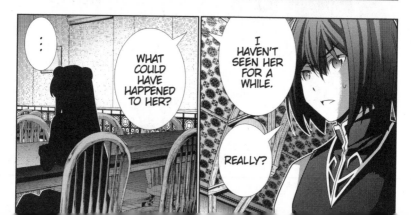

...

WHAT COULD HAVE HAPPENED TO HER?

I HAVEN'T SEEN HER FOR A WHILE.

REALLY?

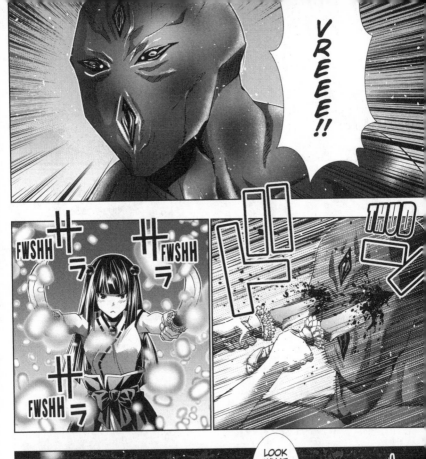

VREEEE!!

FWSHH

FWSHH

FWSHH

THUD

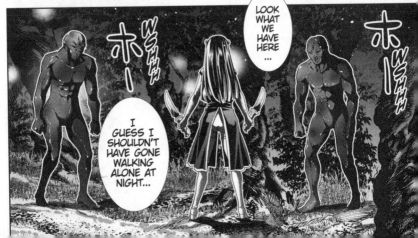

LOOK WHAT WE HAVE HERE...

I GUESS I SHOULDN'T HAVE GONE WALKING ALONE AT NIGHT...

BUT I...
ALSO WANTED TO BE OF USE TO YOTA.
CLASP
RIIIIP
?!
UGH...
SQUEEZE

KA-THUD THWAM

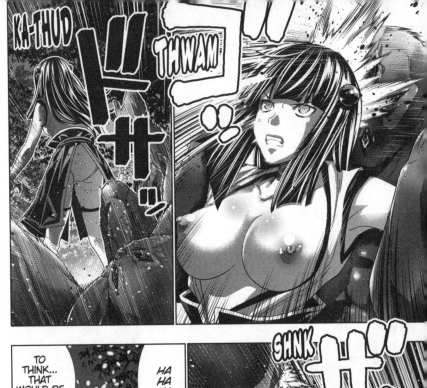

TO
THINK...
THAT
WOULD BE
SO UN-
PLEASANT
...

HA
HA
HA
...

SHNK

SHNK

SHNK

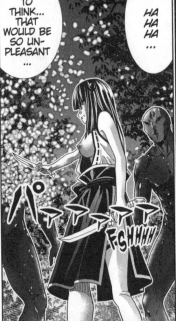

F-SHHHH

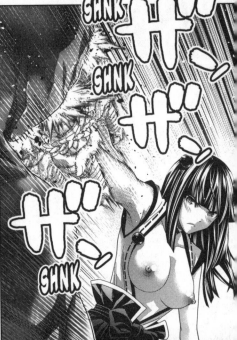

TO BE TOUCHED BY ANY MALE OTHER THAN YOTA...
KER-WHAM
THUD
CLENCH

VREEEEE!
VREEE!
VREEEE!

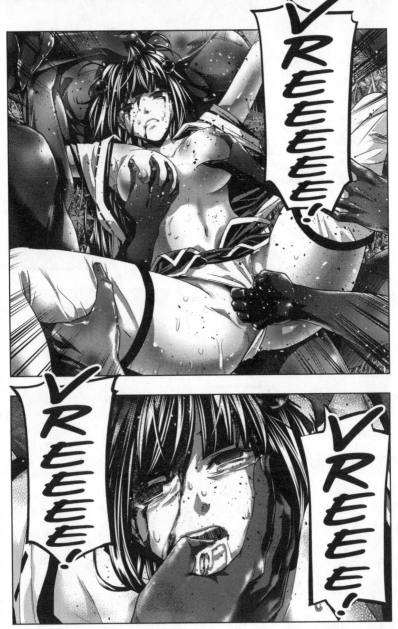

HOW IS IT?

HMMM ...

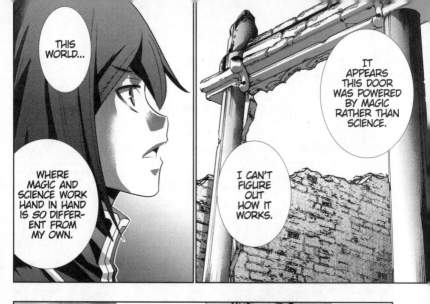

THIS WORLD...

WHERE MAGIC AND SCIENCE WORK HAND IN HAND IS SO DIFFERENT FROM MY OWN.

IT APPEARS THIS DOOR WAS POWERED BY MAGIC RATHER THAN SCIENCE.

I CAN'T FIGURE OUT HOW IT WORKS.

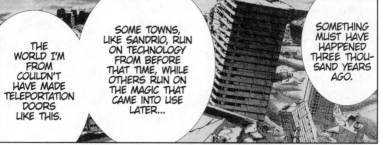

THE WORLD I'M FROM COULDN'T HAVE MADE TELEPORTATION DOORS LIKE THIS.

SOME TOWNS, LIKE SANDRIO, RUN ON TECHNOLOGY FROM BEFORE THAT TIME, WHILE OTHERS RUN ON THE MAGIC THAT CAME INTO USE LATER...

SOMETHING MUST HAVE HAPPENED THREE THOUSAND YEARS AGO.

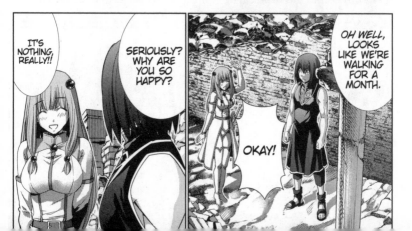

IT'S NOTHING, REALLY!!

SERIOUSLY? WHY ARE YOU SO HAPPY?

OH WELL, LOOKS LIKE WE'RE WALKING FOR A MONTH.

OKAY!

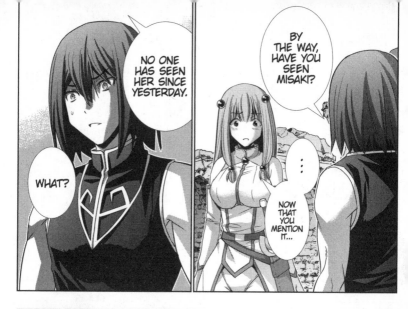

NO ONE HAS SEEN HER SINCE YESTERDAY.

BY THE WAY, HAVE YOU SEEN MISAKI?

WHAT?

⋮

NOW THAT YOU MENTION IT...

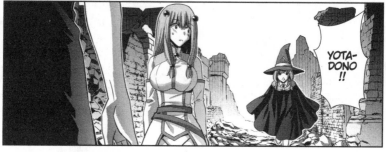

YOTA-DONO!!

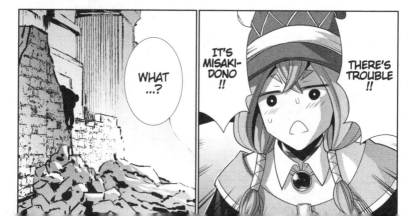

WHAT...?

IT'S MISAKI-DONO!!

THERE'S TROUBLE!!

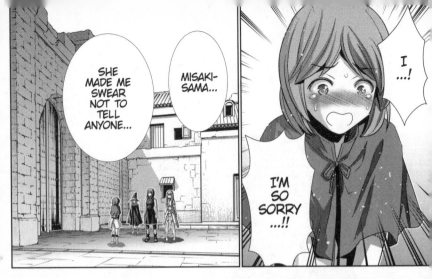

SHE MADE ME SWEAR NOT TO TELL ANYONE...

MISAKI-SAMA...

I ...!

I'M SO SORRY ...!!

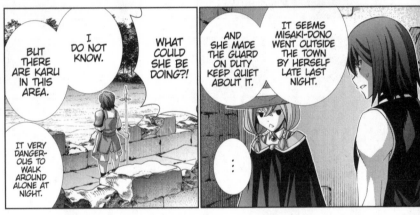

BUT THERE ARE KARU IN THIS AREA.

I DO NOT KNOW.

WHAT COULD SHE BE DOING?!

IT VERY DANGEROUS TO WALK AROUND ALONE AT NIGHT.

AND SHE MADE THE GUARD ON DUTY KEEP QUIET ABOUT IT.

IT SEEMS MISAKI-DONO WENT OUTSIDE THE TOWN BY HERSELF LATE LAST NIGHT.

:

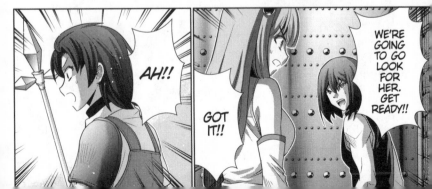

AH!!

WE'RE GOING TO GO LOOK FOR HER. GET READY!!

GOT IT!!

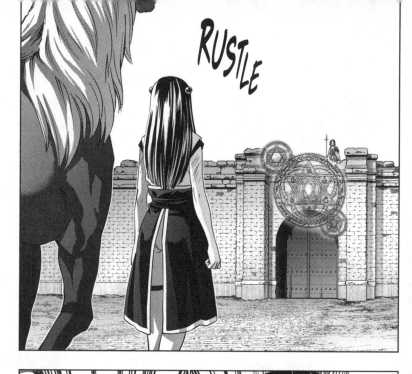

RUSTLE

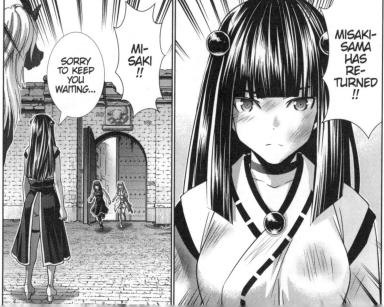

SORRY TO KEEP YOU WAITING...

MI-SAKI!!

MISAKI-SAMA HAS RE-TURNED!!

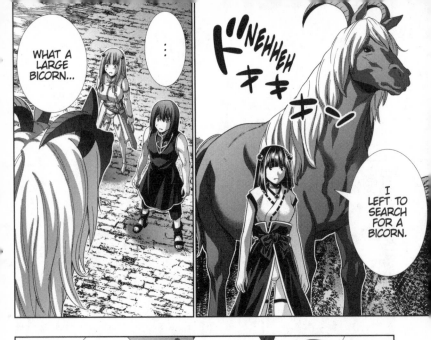

WHAT A LARGE BICORN...

...

NEHHEH

I LEFT TO SEARCH FOR A BICORN.

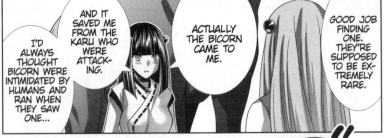

I'D ALWAYS THOUGHT BICORN WERE INTIMIDATED BY HUMANS AND RAN WHEN THEY SAW ONE...

AND IT SAVED ME FROM THE KARU WHO WERE ATTACK-ING.

ACTUALLY THE BICORN CAME TO ME.

GOOD JOB FINDING ONE. THEY'RE SUPPOSED TO BE EX-TREMELY RARE.

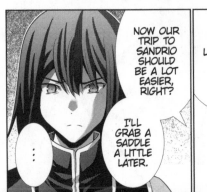

NOW OUR TRIP TO SANDRIO SHOULD BE A LOT EASIER, RIGHT?

...

I'LL GRAB A SADDLE A LITTLE LATER.

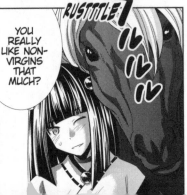

RUSTTTLE

YOU REALLY LIKE NON-VIRGINS THAT MUCH?

きゅくんBLUSH

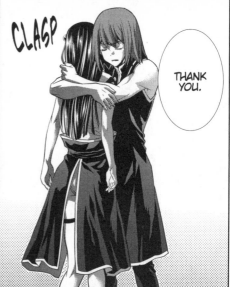

CLASP

THANK YOU.

HA HA HA ...

. . . . .

にゅる DRIBBLE

にゅる DRIBBLE

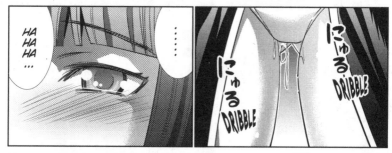

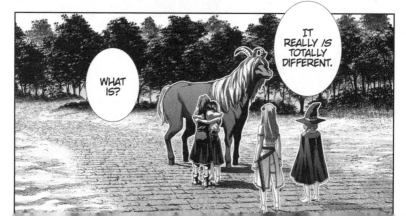

IT REALLY *IS* TOTALLY DIFFERENT.

WHAT IS?

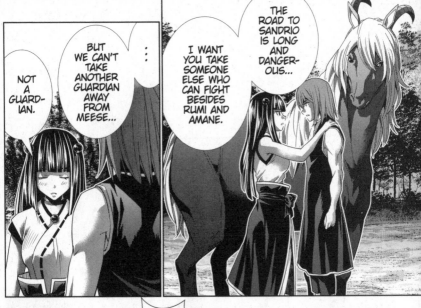

NOT A GUARDIAN.

BUT WE CAN'T TAKE ANOTHER GUARDIAN AWAY FROM MEESE...

I WANT YOU TAKE SOMEONE ELSE WHO CAN FIGHT BESIDES RUMI AND AMANE.

THE ROAD TO SANDRIO IS LONG AND DANGEROUS...

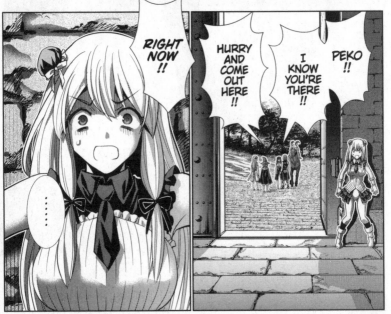

RIGHT NOW!!

HURRY AND COME OUT HERE!!

I KNOW YOU'RE THERE!!

PEKO!!

· · · · ·

PARALLEL
PARADISE

NEXT

ALONG WITH THE DISDAINFUL PEKO, EVERYONE SETS OUT FOR SANDRIO.
PEKO TAKES ON A GROUP OF KARU ALL BY HERSELF!
VREEEEE!!
VREEEEE!!
!!
BOTH HER CHASTITY AND LIFE ARE IN DANGER!!